This book is due for return on or before the last date shown below.

The ULTIMATE MOTORCYCLE BOOK

HUGO WILSON

PHOTOGRAPHY BY DAVE KING

DK

DORLING KINDERSLEY

LONDON · NEW YORK · SYDNEY · MOSCOW

A DORLING KINDERSLEY BOOK

www.dk.com

First published in Great Britain in 1993
by Dorling Kindersley Limited,
9 Henrietta Street, London WC2E 8PS

Art Editor Tracy Hambleton-Miles
Designer Simon Hinchliffe

Project Editor Jane Mason
Editor Laurence Henderson

Managing Editor Sean Moore
Deputy Art Director Tina Vaughan
Deputy Editorial Director Jane Laing

DTP Manager Joanna Figg-Latham
Production Eunice Paterson

2 4 6 8 10 9 7 5 3 1

A CIP catalogue record for this book is
available from the British Library

ISBN 0-7513-0653-3

Reproduced by Colourscan, Singapore
Printed and bound by
C & C Offset in Hong Kong

NOTE ON SPECIFICATION BOXES
*Every effort has been made to ensure that the information supplied in the
specification boxes is accurate. In some cases only estimated values were
available and, in a very few cases, no relevant information existed.
Measurements of individual components and of the motorcycle's weight,
speed, capacity, etc are quoted according to the convention of
the country of origin.*

Contents

Author's Foreword

THE MOTORCYCLE IS the perfect union of two wheels and an internal combustion engine. For more than a hundred years, people have been building, developing, and riding motorcycles. In that time they have evolved from Daimler's machine built of wood, brass, and steel into the powerful and sophisticated bike of today. Motorcycles of all kinds have been built all around the world: from the extraordinary three-seater Böhmerland to the mould-breaking Bimota Tesi; from Soichiro Honda's top-selling 49cc step-through to the all-conquering MV Agusta Grand Prix machines of the fifties and sixties. Motorcycles are more than metal from which they are built; they are the smell of methanol fumes at a speedway meeting, watching the scenery go by on a touring trip, the sound of a V-twin being gunned around the banking at Daytona, and the total satisfaction of firing up your own bike after a nuts-and-bolts rebuild. Bikes can be anything that you want them to be including a means to get to work, a quick way of delivering messages, a way of travelling to far-off places, or one of the most thrilling sports in the world. Above all, motorbikes mean fun. Millions of riders around the world can't be wrong whether they are going to the shops or hurtling along a race track at 200mph. Within these pages you'll find some of the biggest and fastest as well as the smallest and slowest of the world's motorcycles. The ultimate machines demand the Ultimate book: this is it.

The First Motorcycle

THE MOTORCYCLE IS AN AMALGAMATION of two elements, the motor and the bicycle. The invention of the "motorcycle" could not take place until these separate items reached a stage of refinement that allowed them to be combined. The parallel development of the bicycle, with its strong "diamond" pattern frame, and the internal combustion engine reached fruition at an ideal moment to allow the creation of a viable motorized cycle. Enthusiasm for two-wheeled transport swept through Europe and America as the invention captured the public imagination.

The Michaux-Perreaux velocipede
This combination of a small steam engine and a wooden-framed "bone shaker" bicycle was the world's first motorized two-wheeler.

Two-wheeled Transport

Single-track, two-wheeled vehicles first appeared in the late eighteenth century; they had no steering and were propelled by the rider pushing his feet along the ground. When steering was added to the front wheel in 1817, these devices, known as "Hobby-horses", became very popular with the upper classes but as a toy, rather than a true means of transport. A Scottish blacksmith, Kirkpatrick MacMillan, created a cycle with pedals and cranks that drove the rear wheel. He travelled 140 miles (225km) on this device in 1842.

Macmillan's bicycle may have been the first to use pedals, but production of bicycles began in France two decades later. Pierre Michaux fitted cranks to the front wheel of a cycle, later increasing the size of the wheel to improve the gearing. Innovations such as metal-spoked wheels, ball bearings, solid rubber tyres, free wheels, and gears all made bicycles more practical and the arrival of Rover's safety bicycle in 1885 (p.9) inspired the layout for subsequent motorcycle chassis.

Power Sources

The steam engine was invented in the eighteenth century and the first "horseless carriage" was the Cugnot steam wagon of 1770. The power-to-weight ratio of steam engines was poor and the fuel source was bulky. Steam was ideal for stationary engines and for railway locomotives. Small steam engines were designed for commercial purposes and, in 1869, French cycle maker Michaux and engineer Louis-Guillaume Perreaux fitted a small steam engine to a "bone shaker". This machine made a trial run from Paris to St Germain, about ten miles (16km). The makers decided that steam power was better suited to tricycles and did not take the concept further. In America, at almost the same time, Sylvester Roper also built a steam-powered two-wheeler. The American Copeland brothers built a prototype steam-powered "Penny Farthing" bicycle in 1884 and then manufactured powered tricycles commercially. Other means of propulsion were tried. The "Cynophere" was a tricycle equipped with cage-like rear

wheels – dogs ran in the cages to propel the cycle. Another invention used clockwork power but the motor needed rewinding every few hundred yards. In 1897 Humber built a tandem that used electric power but the weight of the batteries was excessive.

The Internal Combustion Engine

The steam engine established the idea of turning gas pressure (steam) into circular motion by the use of cylinder, piston, connecting rod, and crankshaft. Replacing steam pressure with a controlled explosion was a logical move.

The Copeland Steam Bicycle
This steam-powered bicycle was built by the Copeland brothers in Philadelphia in 1894. After experimenting extensively with the two-wheeled prototype they switched to three-wheeled machines, manufacturing a number of steam-powered tricycles.

Gottlieb Daimler
When he left the Deutz company, Gottlieb Daimler began to develop his own four-stroke engine at his workshop in Cannstatt and built the first motorcycle in 1885. He went on to build the successful, prestigious four-wheelers for which the name Daimler is best known.

By the time, Dr Nicholaus Otto patented the four-stroke principle in 1876, the concept of the internal combustion engine was already established. Already a rather impractical car had been built in Dresden. Petrol-powered internal combustion engines were still far from being realistic power units – but the potential was there. Ignition systems were very crude; many used a metal tube inserted into the top of the cylinder. The external end of the tube was sealed and heated until red-hot by a flame. When the piston compressed the charge inside the cylinder some of the mixture was forced up to the red-hot end of the tube where it ignited. Carburettors were even more rudimentary; the fuel/air mixture was created by drawing air across a fuel reservoir, the petrol evaporated and the mixture was sucked into the cylinder.

The First Motorcycle

Otto had an assistant called Gottlieb Daimler who left in 1883 to develop his own internal combustion engine. Daimler mounted his engine into a wooden-framed machine in 1885. It actually had four wheels but history

The Rover Safety Bicycle
The motorcycle chassis can be clearly traced back to Rover's Safety Bicycle built in 1885 by John Kemp Starley. *Chain drive to the rear wheel meant that the wheels could be of similar sizes with the rider seated between them.*

overlooks the two stabilizers and declares this to be the first motorcycle. The engine was positioned vertically in the centre of the machine; drive to the rear wheel was by belt to a counter shaft, then by gear to the rear wheel. A twist grip controlled the rear brake. The exhaust valve was mechanically operated, but the inlet was opened by suction of the piston. The air-cooled Daimler retained a surface carburettor

and hot-tube ignition; the engine ran at 700rpm. On November 10, 1885, Daimler's son Paul rode six miles (9.5km) from Cannstatt to Unterturkheim and back, and became the world's first motorcyclist. Carburation was advanced greatly when Daimler's assistant Maybach invented the spray carburettor. In England, Edward Butler built a a tricycle with electric ignition and a float-feed carburettor in 1887.

The Daimler Motorcycle
Despite its archaic appearance, the Daimler combines many interesting features, including the poppet-valve engine (mechanical exhaust with a suction inlet), twist-grip controls, and a linkage steering system. This machine is a replica, based on Daimler's original drawings.

Ratchet release

Twist-grip control for clutch and brake

Steering linkages

Metal-rimmed wooden wheels

Drive belt tension lever

Exhaust pipe

Fuel reservoir

Tensioning pulley

Counter-shaft pulley

New Engines

EXPERIMENTS WITH the internal combustion engine and two-, three-, and four-wheeled vehicles continued in the 1880s and 1890s; the first motorcycles had run but they were far from perfect. The design of the Rover safety bicycle suggested the layout that motorcycles should adopt for their chassis but the location of the engine was still subject to experiment by designers. The engine also needed further refinement, and above all, more power.

French Motorcycle Pioneers
Rochet and Clement were part of the industry that sprang up on using the De Dion engine; both these firms had vanished by 1910.

The Start of an Industry

The Hildebrand brothers and their associate Alois Wolfmüller had already constructed, and abandoned, steam and two-stroke engines when they built a two-cylinder four-stroke machine in 1894. They installed it in a specially-constructed frame when the conventional bicycle chassis proved to be too weak. The perfected machine was capable of 24mph (38.6km/h) and was offered for sale to the public. The bike was constructed in Munich and also, under licence, in France. The Hildebrand and Wolfmüller had some advanced features; it used water cooling and two cylinders. It also had some severe design problems; connecting rods from the pistons drove directly on to the back wheel making the drive far from smooth at low speeds, and almost impossible at less than 5mph (8km/h). As it had no flywheels, the pistons had to be forced to complete the whole cycle by rubber belts. Production was short-lived because the design was overtaken by developments in France.

The De Dion Engine

Count Albert De Dion and his partner Georges Bouton had been keen enthusiasts about steam power. However in 1884 they turned their attention to petrol engines and built a motor based upon Daimler's original design. It was a 120cc engine with a vacuum inlet valve and a mechanically operated exhaust valve. The rather crude surface carburettor was still employed but it used electric ignition. The crankcases were of alloy and the cylinder head and barrel were cast iron. The flywheels were part of the crankshaft and the whole engine was a neat and compact unit. It was capable of turning over at 1,800rpm (more than double that of the Daimler (p.9) but the cooling was not very efficient and it was prone to severe wear. Yet this is the basis of the modern four-stroke engine. De Dion engines were installed into tricycle frames, with the rear axle driven by gear. Various sizes of engine were built and sold. Firms, many of them French, produced an assortment of tricycles, and the odd two-wheeler, using the De Dion engine.

The Hildebrand and Wolfmüller
The design betrays the influence of the safety bicycle layout. The water-cooled two-cylinder machine was soon outdated by the fast-running De Dion.

Radiator/water cooling tank in rear mudguard

Air intake

Carburettor control

Fuel mixture inlet pipe

Valve springs

Rubber strap

Exhaust

Burner for hot tube ignition

The Drive Mechanism
The crankshaft and camshafts are incorporated in the back wheel. The conrods are attached to cranks on the rear axles and the valves are opened by an eccentric brass ring on the rear wheel.

The Forward-engined Werner
The engine of the Werner was above the front wheel, which did inevitably cause handling problems, especially in slippery road conditions. Despite this drawback, the Werner was significantly better than most machines of the period.

John Boyd Dunlop on an early bicycle.

Without the timely invention of the inflatable tyre in 1888 by John Boyd Dunlop, early motorcyclists would have had an even rougher time.

Others makers copied the engine and built, often identical, versions. Over the following years De Dion engines and those of their imitators were installed in a variety of positions in a wide range of bicycles and tricycles.

The Werner Motorcycle
Expatriate Russian brothers, Michel and Eugene Werner, were among those experimenting with motorcycles in Paris, then a melting-pot for the motor industry. In 1897, they built a machine using a small De Dion-style engine placed above the front wheel which it drove via a twisted rawhide belt. It gave a much smoother ride than the gear drive of the De Dion tricycles. The Werner lay-out placed engine weight on the forks, causing steering problems, especially in wet driving conditions. Although the machine still used hot-tube ignition, it set the standard for motorcycles at the turn of the century. De Dion and similar engines led to the beginning of the motorcycle industry as cycle manufacturers rushed to fit the engines to bicycles. The location of engines varied from within the hubs of wheels to behind the rear wheel, and under the saddle. In 1901 the Werners created a revised design: they split the frame in front of the pedals and bolted the engine into the gap. The frame was strengthened by adding a horizontal member running above the engine. The new layout, with the engine located centrally and low improved weight distribution and resulted in much better handling. The redesigned bikes also boasted electric ignition and a spray-type carburettor. These machines ably dominated the international races of 1902 – the basis for the modern motorcycle had arrived.

1901 Werner
The new Werner moved beyond the bicycle-and-engine concept. The redesigned frame held the engine bolted into place in a gap between the two down-tubes. The addition of a much-improved carburettor, wheelrim brakes, and electric ignition made this one of the first truly practical motorcycles.

Ignition and carburettor controls

Pulley rim rear brake

Vacuum-operated inlet valve

A2201

Twisted rawhide drive belt

Cast iron cylinder barrel

Alloy crank cases

On the Road

THE 1901 WERNER provided the realistic starting point for the evolution of the modern motorcycle. Its engine became the established benchmark of performance and construction, and the chassis determined the most viable position for the engine. There was still a long process of experimentation and improvement to be completed before the "modern motorcycle" arrived, but in less than fifteen years the machine had evolved from an enthusiast's indulgent fancy into a reasonably practical road-going machine.

Racing at Brooklands
By the turn of the century motorcycles were being raced and competition helped to evaluate new developments and to spread new ideas. British racers benefited from the world's first purpose-built race track when the Brooklands circuit opened in 1907, the year after racing had begun on public roads in the Isle of Man.

Riding the First Motorcycles

The 1901 Werner was a vast improvement upon its predecessors, but that is only a reflection on the primitive nature of early bikes. The improved machine was still difficult to ride. It had no clutch, so the engine could not be kept running if the machine was stationary. The brakes were extremely inefficient. Insufficient power meant that the bike was unable to climb a hill that was more than a slight incline without the rider having to resort to pedalling. The bike had no suspension so it shook itself, and its rider, to pieces. The vacuum-operated inlet valves stuck open and belts slipped in less than ideal conditions. The roads were awful and finding petrol could be difficult. Only simple bicycle lights were available for night riders. In the next thirteen years roads improved a little but bikes made great advances. By 1903, motorcycles were being designed and manufactured all over Europe and in America. Some had built their own engines but many bought in proprietary motors. There was no logical pattern to the development of the bikes during this period. Some basic problems were common to all machines and designers developed or borrowed solutions. Front suspension was adopted widely, yet many designers thought that rear suspension was unnecessary and that it put undue strain on the drive chain.

Critical Developments

A number of crucial advances occurred in the period up to 1914. Electric battery and coil ignition replaced the hot-tube system used on the earliest engines but, at the turn of the century, batteries were very unreliable. André Boudeville invented a high-tension magneto in 1898. Although its design was not perfected for another five years, by 1906 it was almost universal.

The FN Motorcycle

FN designer Paul Kelecom used a four-cylinder engine to reduce vibration. The motor was coupled to a shaft-drive transmission, with no clutch or gearbox. The machine also featured a drum rear brake and leading-link forks. The design was so advanced that production continued for over twenty years though later models were fitted with a clutch and gearbox.

Throttle

The manual oil pump is operated by the rider

Rear drum brake, no front brake is fitted

Bevel gear casing for shaft drive

The engine is suspended from between the frame rails

Magneto is driven from the end of the crankshaft

Leading-link forks were the most simple form of front suspension

The Two-stroke Scott
The first of the Yorkshire-built Scotts appeared in 1905. Its most notable feature was the extraordinary water-cooled two-stroke engine but the bike also used telescopic forks, all-chain transmission including a two-speed gear ratio and a kick-starter. Pedals were not considered necessary.

Oil pump
Water cooling radiator
Centrally sprung telescopic forks
Bicycle-style stirrup brakes
Magneto ignition
Carburettor air intake
Kickstart pedal

Gear Selection Pedal
Early gearboxes required considerable ingenuity on the part of designers. Scott adopted a two-speed design that used two separate primary drive ratios, selected by the foot pedal.

The spray carburettor, fed from a float chamber, was improved over this period but most makers bought in these specialized components. However the quality of the carburettors is indicated by the fact that many machines relied upon the ignition timing or even variations of valve lift to control engine speed! Leading-link forks, that could often be bolted to existing solid forks, supplied front suspension. Telescopic forks adopted on the Scott were a notable advance. There was universal agreement that transmission needed

improving over the belt-driven machines with a single gear and no clutch. A clutch allowed the use of harsher, but more efficient chain drive, and gearboxes were adopted by many firms, though others like Terrot (p.137) and Rudge (p.87) developed belt drive systems with a variable pulley size. Shaft drive was adopted for very few machines. Engine controls were often awkwardly positioned on early machines but the Bowden control cable brought twist-grip throttle and handlebar-mounted levers into common

usage, making machines easier to control. Better understanding of engine efficiency, helped achieve increased power outputs, which would reveal deficiencies in other components, and the cycle of improvements began again.

Into the Future
By 1914, the constituents of a modern motorcycle had been used with varying degrees of success. Over the following eighty years, the amazing factor is not how much motorcycles improved, but how little they have changed.

1913 Award-winning Sunbeam
Sunbeam (p.86) built their first machines in 1913 and scored a resounding success in that year's International Six Days Trial (p.157) and became famous for fine quality.

1914 Indian V-twin
Indians were well designed and well constructed motorcycles that included many advanced features. Even very early machines used all-chain transmission and twist-grip controls. This 1914 model has rear suspension, a two-speed gearbox, a speedometer, and electric lighting. A version was also built with an electric starter.

Indian were among the first to adopt twist grip controls
Electric lighting
Rear suspension spring

The World's Motorcycles

MOTORCYCLES ARE BUILT all over the world, from Brazil to Byelorussia, Germany to Japan. Over a hundred years of motorcycle history, industries have come and gone, but many of the infinite variety of machines that they made survive in museums, or in the hands of private enthusiasts.

America

The American motorcycle industry has been dominated by one engine type for over eighty years: the V-twin.

As in Europe, when motorized transport captured the public imagination, many small companies began making powered two-wheelers. The first American motorcycles appeared at the turn of the century and quality varied enormously. Pioneer American motorcyclists needed rugged, reliable machines able to cover great distances on rough roads. Manufacturers responded by producing strong, simple, large-capacity machines. Technology progressed rapidly: Royal built a chain-drive two-speed machine in 1902. Indian (pp.34-9) introduced rear suspension in 1913, the same year that Cyclone built their overhead-camshaft V-twin. By 1914, over thirty makes of motorcycle were in production, sales were buoyant, and the future seemed bright for the industry. Indian, whose products were exported worldwide, were the biggest manufacturer in the world.

The Ace logo

The Classic American V-twin
By 1914 the V-twin was established as the most popular American motorcycle engine, a position that it still retains. Harley-Davidson (pp.18-27), Indian, Excelsior (p.41), and others all adopted this engine layout. Competition within the industry was fierce, but competition also came increasingly from the motor car, in particular from Henry Ford's Model T, introduced in 1908. The Model T became cheaper as production increased, so that in a few years they were less expensive than many motorcycles. By the mid-twenties, the number of significant motorcycle manufacturers had shrunk to just three. Indian were still the largest company, followed by Harley-Davidson; Excelsior, whose machines were built in Chicago by the Schwinn bicycle company, were the smallest. Production at Excelsior halted abruptly in 1931 with the onset of the Great Depression. Harley-Davidson and Indian were left to fight for the home market. Still controlled by the founders, Harley were not bound by the demands of share holders. Indian, by contrast, were more interested in short-term profit and therefore invested much less in developing new models. By the late thirties, Harley had taken the leading position

The Ace Trophy

in home sales. By the end of the Second World War, Harley had achieved financial success and consolidated a clear market advantage.

Illuminated Indian mudguard motif

Competition from Abroad
In the late 1940s, machines imported from England began to flood the market. British bikes were lighter, faster, and more sporty than the domestic machines. Indian, now under new ownership, attempted to revive its fortunes by producing a similar style of machine. A great deal of money was invested in this new venture but it ended in disaster. The new bikes were uncompetitive and unreliable. The final insult was that after production in America ceased the Indian name was attached to an assortment of machines built abroad. From 1959, machines from Japan and Britain continued to flood on to the American market. The Japanese concentrated on small-capacity machines that sold well. In an attempt to counter the Japanese challenge, Harley then took an interest in the Italian company, Aermacchi, and began selling these smaller-capacity bikes in America, under the Harley-Davidson name. From 1960 until 1977, lightweight Harleys were also built at Aermacchi's factory.

Schrader balloon tyre pressure gauge

1960 Harley-Davidson Duo Glide

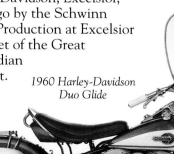

Harley-Davidson's Heritage
Harley-Davidson had merged with American Machine & Foundry Inc. in 1969; AMF had capital and resources, but quality control was poor. In 1981, Harley management bought the company back. A decade of financial difficulties followed, combined with increased demand and improved machines. By the late eighties, they had staged a dramatic recovery; the basis of Harley's successful revival was their proud past and the vogue for nostalgia. Eighty years of manufacturing history endorsed every motorcycle sold.

The First Harley

WILLIAM S. HARLEY and his school friend Arthur Davidson began experimenting with internal combustion engines at the turn of the century. Harley worked as a draughtsman for an engineering company; Davidson was employed as a pattern maker. Together they constructed a simple 25cu. in (400cc) single-cylinder engine and fitted it to a bicycle frame; the prototype was completed in 1903. When tested, the machine proved to be reliable, but underpowered. Harley redesigned the engine and increased its capacity to 35cu. in (475cc). The Harley-Davidson Motor Company began production with the "Silent Gray Fellow" in 1904. In the next 14 years design modifications increased engine capacity again, included inlet-over-exhaust valvegear, and strengthened the frame.

Founding brothers, William A. Davidson, Walter Davidson, Sr., Arthur Davidson, and William S. Harley formed the Harley-Davidson company. Their first workshop was a wooden shed in the back yard of the Davidson family home.

1912 Harley-Davidson Silent Gray Fellow
Named "Silent" because efficient mufflers promoted quiet motorcycling, "Gray" for the bike's austere paintwork, and "Fellow" to suggest a reliable partnership between man and machine, this bike had a reputation for being a trusted companion on the road.

Full loop construction gives the frame additional strength

Pedals start the engine and set the bike in motion because it has no starter or gearbox

Drive is transmitted from the engine of the Silent Gray Fellow to the rear wheel by a leather belt. Tensioned belt drives were unreliable and were soon abandoned. By 1919 Harley-Davidson had fitted all their bikes with a clutch, chain drive, and a gearbox.

German Bosch Magneto

Free wheel clutch is operated by lever

Tensioned belt drive creates a crude clutch.

An atmospheric inlet valve is opened by the vacuum in the cylinder

Sober grey paint-work contributed to the bike's name

The leading-link fork was adopted soon after production began. The same design, developed and refined, was used until the introduction of the telescopic fork on the first Hydra-Glide (p.27) in 1949

SPECIFICATIONS

Silent Gray Fellow

- **ENGINE** Single cylinder inlet-over-exhaust engine
- **BORE AND STROKE** 3³⁄₁₆ x 3½in (84 x 89mm)
- **CAPACITY** 30cu. in (494cc)
- **POWER OUTPUT** 6½bhp
- **CARBURATION** Schebler carburettors
- **IGNITION** Bosch magneto
- **TRANSMISSION** Single-speed belt drive
- **CLUTCH** Belt idler
- **FRAME** Tubular loop
- **SUSPENSION** Leading-link forks, rigid rear
- **BRAKES** Rear wheel coaster brake (Back-pedal brake)
- **WEIGHT** 195lb (88.5kg)
- **TOP SPEED** 45mph (72kmh)
- **YEAR OF CONSTRUCTION** 1912
- An acetylene Prest-O-Light is fitted.

Schebler carburettor. Until 1909 Harley-Davidson made their own carburettors – legend has it that an early prototype was designed using an empty tin of tomatoes

Harley-Davidson

In 1907 HARLEY-DAVIDSON built their first V-twin. To build and develop V-twins was quite straightforward and many companies experimented with the design. A single-cylinder machine could easily be adapted to produce a simple V-twin that delivered twice as much power. The frame could usually remain the same; only the crankcases needed serious redesigning. The design was a success and Harley stuck with it. Harley are still building V-twins, to the same 45° layout, and the V-twin engine has come to be regarded as the classic American motorcycle engine.

SPECIFICATIONS

1915 Harley-Davidson J-11
- **ENGINE** Inlet-over-exhaust two-cylinder V-twin
- **CAPACITY** 60cu.in (989cc)
- **POWER OUTPUT** 11bhp @ 7,200rpm
- **TRANSMISSION** Three-speed gearbox, chain drive
- **FRAME** Loop `
- **SUSPENSION** Leading-link forks
- **WEIGHT** 325lb (147.5kg)
- **TOP SPEED** 60mph (96.5km/h)

1915 Harley-Davidson J-11
By 1915 Harley-Davidson's development of the V-twin was well advanced. The similarity between the engines of the single and the twin are obvious, though the twin has a mechanical inlet valve. The inlet-over-exhaust layout was retained on the big twins until 1929.

Spark plugs were fitted into the valve pocket of the engine

CR 4732

Oil feed inspection window

This 1915 model was the last to feature pedal starting

A three-speed hand-change gearbox was introduced in 1915

SPECIFICATIONS

1926 BA Peashooter
- **ENGINE** Overhead-valve single-cylinder
- **CAPACITY** 21cu. in (346cc)
- **POWER OUTPUT** 10bhp
- **TRANSMISSION** Three-speed gearbox, chain drive
- **FRAME** Tubular steel loop
- **SUSPENSION** Springer leading-link forks
- **WEIGHT** 263lb (119kg)
- **TOP SPEED** 60mph (96.5km/h)

1926 Harley-Davidson BA Peashooter
In 1926 Harley introduced a new range of small single-cylinder bikes, available as a side-valve or overhead-valve machines, that became known as "Peashooters" because of the sound their engines made. These bikes continued in production until 1934.

Olive green was the standard paint finish for the American home market

The first Yank and Harley to enter Germany. 11/12/18

"The first Yank ..."
This famous photograph shows Corporal Holtz, the first US soldier into Germany after the First World War on a Harley.

1941 Harley-Davidson WL

A range of 45cu. in (737cc) side-valve V-twins was unveiled in 1928 to compete with the Indian Scout (p.36) and the Excelsior Super-X (p.41). The smaller twins became known as "Forty-fives" to differentiate them from the "Big Twins" with 61 or 74cu. in (1000 or 1213cc) engines. Today's Harleys developed from the "Forty-fives".

Front side light

The left side of the tank holds oil, the right side is for petrol

The paintwork is "Skyway Blue"

Smaller wheels with fat tyres improved the ride

The side-valve engine formed the basis for post-war racers

1942 Harley-Davidson WLA

The simple and rugged "Forty-five" was an ideal military motorcycle. Based on the civilian machine, the Army version was cheaper, stronger, and just as reliable. Over 90,000 WLAs were produced for Allied forces during the Second World War. Harley won the majority of Army contracts for motorcycles and emerged with honour, and finances, in good order.

SPECIFICATIONS

1941 Harley-Davidson WLD
- **ENGINE** Side-valve 45° two-cylinder V-twin
- **CAPACITY** 45cu. in (737cc)
- **POWER OUTPUT** 25bhp (estimated)
- **TRANSMISSION** Three-speed hand-change gearbox, chain drive
- **FRAME** Tubular cradle
- **SUSPENSION** Leading-link springer forks
- **WEIGHT** 530lb (240.4kg)
- **TOP SPEED** 80mph (129km/h) (estimated)

The daunting front aspect of the Army WLA.

SPECIFICATIONS

1942 Harley-Davidson WLA
- **ENGINE** Side-valve 45° V-twin
- **CAPACITY** 45cu.in (737cc)
- **POWER OUTPUT** 23bhp @ 4,600rpm
- **TRANSMISSION** Three-speed gearbox, chain drive
- **FRAME** Tubular cradle
- **SUSPENSION** Leading-link forks
- **WEIGHT** 576lb (261.5kg)
- **TOP SPEED** 65mph (105km/h)

Thompson 45mm calibre machine gun

Canvas fairing and leg shield

Army tail lights have black-out covers fitted.

The forward-mounted saddle follows military specifications

Blackout light

Tyre pump

Extended bash plate

Harley-Davidson Racers

HARLEY-DAVIDSON MADE THEIR DEBUT in motorcycle sport in 1909, when Walter Davidson, on an early single-cylinder machine, entered the Long Island Reliability Run, and achieved a perfect score. The publicity generated by the success convinced the company as to the merits of a competition programme. In the years that followed, Harleys appeared at every kind of sporting event from board tracks to road races. Originally their opposition came from Indian and Excelsior, followed for a time by British bikes. Although Japanese machines now dominate many forms of motorcycle sport, on the dirt tracks of America, Harley are still top dog.

A 1930s American hillclimbing course marked in 50-foot (15m) intervals.

1930 Harley-Davidson Hillclimber
Low gearing enables the bike to climb more steeply. A long, low chassis reduces the machine's centre of gravity and keeps the weight at the front of the bike.

A large fuel tank is not necessary for short climbs

Hillclimbers aim to achieve maximum height or the fastest time on each run.

Chains give the rear wheel extra grip

Sloping footboards keep the rider's weight forward

J-series engine especially tuned for hillclimbing

SPECIFICATIONS

1929 Harley Hillclimber
- **ENGINE** Double overhead-valve V-twin
- **CAPACITY** 74cu. in (1213cc)
- **POWER OUTPUT** Not available
- **TRANSMISSION** Competition single-speed gearbox
- **FRAME** Tubular cradle
- **SUSPENSION** Leading-link forks, rigid rear
- **WEIGHT** 350lb (147kg) (estimated)
- **TOP SPEED** Determined by the gearing chosen for the hillclimb course.

Daytona 200 race winner's flag, 1961

1961 Daytona souvenir racing programme

Clip-on handlebars are used on the long straights to reduce drag

SPECIFICATIONS

1968 Harley-Davidson XR750
- **ENGINE** Overhead-valve 45° V-twin
- **CAPACITY** 750cc
- **POWER OUTPUT** 62bhp (untuned)
- **TRANSMISSION** Four-speed gearbox, chain drive
- **FRAME** Tubular cradle
- **SUSPENSION** Telescopic forks, rear swingarm
- **WEIGHT** 320lb (145kg)
- **TOP SPEED** 145mph (233.5km/h) at Daytona in 1970

1968 Harley-Davidson XR750

As well as dominating flat-track racing, XR750s with the addition of a fairing and front brakes made very successful road racers. Cal Rayborn won the 1972 and 1973 Transatlantic match races on this machine.

Sculpted fuel tank allows the rider to "tuck in"

Cal Rayborn, one of the greatest riders of his era, died in 1973 racing a Suzuki in New Zealand.

Carburettors run without air cleaners to increase power

Fairing painted in Harley-Davidson racing colours

Rear disc brake as used on the flat-track bike

Leading-shoe drum brake

The flag goes down on Roger Reiman in the 1961 Daytona 200-mile race.

1961 Harley-Davidson KR750

From 1952 until 1968, the KR was the racing Harley. This bike, ridden by Roger Reiman, won the 1961 Daytona 200-mile road race. Although road bikes stopped using side-valve engines in 1955, development of the KR continued until a rule change forced Harley to introduce the overhead-valve XR engine in 1968.

SPECIFICATIONS

1961 Harley-Davidson KR750
- **ENGINE** Overhead-valve 45° V-twin
- **CAPACITY** 750cc
- **POWER OUTPUT** 50bhp
- **TRANSMISSION** Four-speed gearbox, chain drive
- **FRAME** Tubular cradle
- **SUSPENSION** Telescopic forks, rear swingarm
- **WEIGHT** 320lb (145kg)
- **TOP SPEED** 125mph (233km/h)

Traditional Harley side-valve engine

The brake pedal has been drilled to reduce weight

The tyre is screwed to the wheel rim for added security

Daytona 200 winner's trophy

Harley-Davidson 61E

H ARLEY-DAVIDSON BUILT strong dependable machines that they improved year-by-year. Their approach to development was traditionally conservative until 1936, when they introduced a radically new motorcycle. For the first time they built a machine designed with an overhead-valve construction. Previous overhead-valve Harleys were created by adding a new top end to an existing inlet-over-exhaust or side-valve design. The new bike had only one camshaft and hemispherical combustion chambers. A recirculating lubrication system improved the engine's reliability and reduced oil consumption. The styling was radical too: a rounded tank, curving mudguards, instrument console, and the compact look of the machine set the style for future Harleys. With the 61E, Harley-Davidson took the lead in American bike design.

Joe Petrali, on a tuned 61, created an Ocean-level land-speed record of 136mph (219km/h) in March 1937.

Gear lever

Horn

Foot operated clutch lever

A front view of the 61E.

1936 Harley-Davidson Knucklehead 61E

The 61E is the most important bike in Harley-Davidson history, the first of the big twins to employ overhead valves and a recirculating lubrication system, and the direct ancestor of today's Harleys. It offered a level of performance and style that was so far ahead of its rival, the Indian Chief (pp.38-9), that, although Indian survived for another fifteen years, they never recovered the technological lead. The 61E was a high-tech motorcycle in 1936 and established the look for all subsequent Harleys.

The oil tank wraps around the battery

Air-flow tail light

Main stand mounted on rear of rigid frame

Burgess fishtail muffler

Four-speed constant mesh gearbox

The overhead-valve engine introduced on the Harley-Davidson model 61 was nicknamed the "Knucklehead" because the engine had the appearance of the back of a clenched fist. The rocker covers form the "knuckles".

Speedometer

Reserve tank

Main tank

Ammeter

Oil pressure markers

Light switch

The tank-top console of controls and gauges are designed for maximum efficiency and clarity.

SPECIFICATIONS

Harley-Davidson 61E

- •**ENGINE** Overhead-valve 45° V-twin
- •**BORE AND STROKE** 3³⁄₁₆ x 3½ in (83 x 89mm)
- •**CAPACITY** 61cu. in (989cc)
- •**POWER OUTPUT** 37bhp @ 4,800rpm
- •**CARBURATION** Linkert carburettors
- •**IGNITION** Battery and coil
- •**TRANSMISSION** Four-speed handchange gearbox, chain drive
- •**CLUTCH** Dry multiplate
- •**FRAME** Tubular cradle
- •**SUSPENSION** Leading-link forks
- •**BRAKES** Drum brakes, front and rear
- •**WEIGHT** 515lb (234kg)
- •**TOP SPEED** 100mph (161km/h)
- •**YEAR OF CONSTRUCTION** 1936

Harley used many different motifs. This design was used in the late 1930s

Forks used tubular legs instead of the I-beams used on side-valve models

Front and rear wheels are interchangeable, a common feature of motorcycles at this time

Contact breaker case

This style of air filter was fitted for one year only

Screws regulate the oil pump's delivery rate

The overhead-valve design needed only one camshaft

Harley-Davidson Glides

WHEN INDIAN CEASED PRODUCTION in 1953, Harley-Davidson's competition came from abroad; lighter, faster, British machines, with better handling, flooded the American market. In the sixties, fast, powerful, and reliable Japanese motorcycles followed the British and won over American bike buyers. In response, Harley turned to the nostalgia market, making traditional looks their hallmark. This strategy brought Harley-Davidson into the 1990s as one of the select few manufacturers increasing market share and production.

SPECIFICATIONS

1960 FLH Duo Glide
- **ENGINE** Overhead-valve 45° V-twin
- **CAPACITY** 74cu. in (1213cc)
- **POWER OUTPUT** 55bhp @ 7200rpm
- **TRANSMISSION** Four-speed gearbox, chain drive
- **FRAME** Tubular steel cradle
- **SUSPENSION** Telescopic forks, rear swingarm
- **WEIGHT** 670lb (304kg)
- **TOP SPEED** 100mph (160km/h)

1960 FLH Duo Glide
The FLH Duo Glide, a powerful, luxurious machine, became known worldwide as the traditional American touring bike. Most customers had their big Harleys fitted with panniers and large windshields.

Knurled petrol cap

Rear shock absorbers

Panniers were supplied as optional extras

Plump white-walled tyres added to the rider's comfort and to the bike's flamboyant looks

Exhausts have chrome covers

This splendid trumpet horn was fitted as a standard feature

1987 FLHS Electra Glide
The Electra Glide was introduced in 1965. Harley-Davidson had at last produced a motorcycle with an electric starter – fifty years after Indian made their first attempts to do so. The Electra Glide is still in production.

Many modern Harleys use toothed-belt final drive

Twin front discs

— DID YOU KNOW? —
In October 1970, Harley rider Cal Rayborn became the fastest man on two wheels. His cigar-shaped machine powered by a tuned Sportster engine achieved a speed of 265.5mph (427.2km/h) on Bonneville Salt Flats.

1949 FL Hydra Glide
- **ENGINE** Overhead-valve 45° V-twin
- **CAPACITY** 74cu. in (1213cc)
- **POWER OUTPUT** 55bhp @ 7200rpm
- **TRANSMISSION** Four-speed gearbox, chain drive
- **FRAME** Tubular steel cradle
- **SUSPENSION** Telescopic forks
- **WEIGHT** 590lb (268kg)
- **TOP SPEED** 102mph (164km/h)

1949 FL Hydra Glide

For the Hydra Glide, Harley-Davidson abandoned Springer forks, replacing them with improved, hydraulically damped telescopic forks. Springers had been used on Harleys since 1907 and did continue to be used. These new machines, christened "Hydra Glides", used the Panhead motor that replaced the Knucklehead 61E (pp.24-5).

Sprung seat posts were originally used by Harley in 1912

Hydraulically damped telescopic forks

Panhead engine

Typically large bulbous headlight

Additional side lights

Skirted "air-flow" fenders

This Duo Glide features many period accessories, such as the elaborate front mudguard detailing

Customized leather panniers

Kickstart return spring

Ignition timing unit

Crash bars protect the engine

Sixties advertising focuses on the fun and freedom of motorcycling.

Single front drum-brake

The Duo-Glide Rider's Handbook formed part of Harley-Davidson's after-sales advice and maintenance schemes.

Harley's famous Milwaukee factory is seen here (above).

1988 FLHS Electra Glide

The rubber-mounted Evolution engine looks similar to earlier types but improves reliability and is much easier to maintain. Traditional looks are retained but the bike is now more user-friendly.

The gearbox is a separate unit

Fog lamps

Disc brakes were first fitted in 1972

1987/8 FLHS Electra Glide
- **ENGINE** Overhead-valve 45° V-twin
- **CAPACITY** 82cu.in (1340cc)
- **POWER OUTPUT** 55bhp @ 7200rpm
- **TRANSMISSION** Five-speed gearbox, belt drive
- **FRAME** Tubular steel cradle
- **SUSPENSION** Telescopic forks, twin shock absorber swingarm
- **WEIGHT** 692lb (314kg)
- **TOP SPEED** 100mph (161km/h)

Police Motorcycles

T HE PERFORMANCE AND MANOEUVRABILITY of a powerful motorcycle make it ideal for police purposes, and in a chase in urban areas, a bike is especially useful. In addition, good handling at low-speed is important, so lighter twin-cylinder machines are often favoured over faster but more cumbersome fours. Police bikes are specially adapted machines to carry radios, sirens, and additional lights. Competition for the lucrative police market has always been keen: European forces favoured BMW machines in the seventies and eighties; American police are reverting to the traditional Harley.

Police riders demonstrate their consummate skills.

This 1951 Harley was used by the Willowick Ohio Police Department for 36 years.

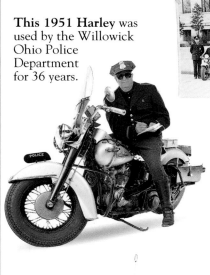

Police Harleys could apprehend even a speed machine such as this Harley Big Twin.

A Police department assembles with its complement of Harley motorcycles and three-wheeler Servi-car (centre).

1951 Harley-Davidson FL
Based upon the older Hydra-Glide model (p.27), this machine is typical of American police motorcycles that were used during the forties and fifties. Today, many American Police departments are purchasing Harleys for their patrolmen, after favouring other makes for some years. This positive support has helped Harley in their bid to corner the nostalgia market.

Parking ticket book

Mudguard-mounted fire extinguisher

First-aid kit

Radio equipment

1966 Triumph Saint

The "Saint" (the name was said to stand for "Stops Anything In No Time") was a Police-specification version of Triumph's single-carburettor 650cc model. These bikes were popular with British Police forces from the early fifties until the mid-seventies, when they were replaced with BMW machines.

SPECIFICATIONS

1966 Triumph Saint
- ENGINE Overhead-valve vertical twin
- CAPACITY 647cc
- POWER OUTPUT 40bhp @ 6,500rpm
- TRANSMISSION Four-speed, chain drive
- FRAME Tubular steel cradle
- SUSPENSION Telescopic forks, twin-shock rear swingarm
- WEIGHT 400lb (181kg)
- TOP SPEED 108mph (174km/h)

The blue police identification light is mounted prominently in the centre of the fairing.

Telephone-style radio handset

Solo saddles were specified for police bikes

Illuminated "Police" sign

Red pursuit lights

Legshields are mounted on the crash bars

Primary drive chain case

Fire extinguisher

Mudguard-mounted Police sign

POLICE

SPECIFICATIONS

1951 Harley-Davidson FL
- ENGINE Overhead-valve 45° V-twin
- CAPACITY 74cu.in. (1213cc)
- POWER OUTPUT 55hp
- TRANSMISSION Four-speed with hand gearchange, chain drive
- FRAME Tubular steel cradle
- SUSPENSION Telescopic forks, sprung seat, rigid rear
- WEIGHT 598lb (271kg)
- TOP SPEED 102mph (164km/h) (est)

"Calling all cars, calling all cars !" A patrolman radios in his information. His bike is an early version of the Triumph Saint and has an unsprung frame.

more effective police power with HARLEY-DAVIDSON motorcycles

On guard for safety! Control peak traffic with officers mounted on HARLEY-DAVIDSON

Police sales were potentially profitable and image-enhancing: Harley eagerly sought them with special promotion campaigns.

Police bikes are often used for official state escort duties. In this picture from the fifties, Triumph-mounted officers wait to escort a dignitary from Claridges Hotel in London, England.

Henderson

William G. Henderson, designer of the Henderson, died in a motorcycle accident in 1922.

Hendersons were luxurious, powerful machines, capable of covering great distances with speed and comfort. For performance and refinement they easily outclassed rival machines in the 1920s. Ignatz Schwinn, manufacturer of bicycles and the Excelsior motorcycle (p.41), bought the company in 1917 and Bill Henderson left to set up ACE motorcycles. As the Depression worsened in 1931, Schwinn was forced to halt production. Sadly, it never restarted.

SPECIFICATIONS

1912 Henderson
- **ENGINE** In-line, inlet-over-exhaust, four cylinder
- **CAPACITY** 56cu. in (920cc)
- **POWER OUTPUT** 8hp (estimated)
- **TRANSMISSION** Single-speed, shaft final drive
- **FRAME** Tubular steel cradle
- **SUSPENSION** Leading-axle forks
- **WEIGHT** 295lb (134kg)
- **TOP SPEED** 60mph (96.5km/h)
- Optional passenger seat

1912 Henderson
The revolutionary new Henderson had an exceptionally long wheelbase, and an optional passenger seat installed in front of the rider if required.

Oil is stored in the rear of the fuel tank

Tool bag

Bicycle type saddle

Acetylene tank for lights

Petrol tap

Main stand

Schebler carburettor

Pushrods for mechanical inlet valves

Both pedals operate the same rear brake

A hand starting crank was a new feature. In 1912, most machines still had to be started by vigorous pedalling.

1920 Henderson K
The advanced Henderson K model featured a fully enclosed chain and a pressure lubrication system. Other sophistications included electric lighting, which was fitted as standard.

Tool box

Trailing link forks

Horn button

An enclosed chain improves chain life

SPECIFICATIONS

1920 Henderson K
- **ENGINE** In-line inlet-over-exhaust four cylinder
- **CAPACITY** 80cu. in (1300cc)
- **POWER OUTPUT** 28bhp @ 3400rpm
- **TRANSMISSION** Three-speed gearbox, chain drive
- **FRAME** Tubular steel cradle
- **SUSPENSION** Excelsior Kushion forks
- **WEIGHT** 450lb (204 kg)
- **TOP SPEED** 80mph (129km/h)
- Original design by Arthur O. Lemon.

SPECIFICATIONS

1929 Henderson KJ
- **ENGINE** In-line, inlet-over-exhaust, four cylinder
- **CAPACITY** 79.4cu. in. (1300cc)
- **POWER OUTPUT** 40bhp
- **TRANSMISSION** Three-speed gearbox, with reverse gear, chain drive
- **FRAME** Twin down-tube cradle
- **SUSPENSION** Leading axle forks
- **WEIGHT** 500lb (227kg) (estimated)
- **TOP SPEED** 100mph (160km/h)
- Design by A.R. Constantine

1929 Henderson KJ
Known as the "Streamline", the KJ was an original design based on a familiar layout. Overheating of the rear cylinders was reduced on the five-bearing engine, through improved air cooling.

Light to illuminate instruments

Headlight

Leading-link forks

Speedometer drive

Sprung forks with enclosed central spring

Battery box | Oil feed pipe | Brake pedal | Sidecar mounting lugs | Drum brake

Contemporary opinion stated, as here, that the Henderson K was "the most highly developed motorcycle ever built".

THE ACE MOTORCYCLE

Bill Henderson remained at his old company for only a short time after he sold the firm to Schwinn in 1917. Henderson went on to develop a new machine with a large-capacity four-cylinder engine with chain drive, similar to his Henderson layout, under the ACE name.

When Bill Henderson was killed on a test-ride in 1922, Arthur O. Lemon moved to ACE and again took over where Henderson had left off. Rights to the ACE designs were bought by Indian in 1927 (p.37). Four-cylinder machines based on ACE motorcycles continued in production until 1943.

SPECIAL 1923 ACE XP-4
One of two specially tuned machines built by ACE in 1923, this machine, ridden by Red Wolverton, established a record speed of 130mph (210km/h).

ACE SPEED TROPHY
ACE challenged other makers to beat the XP-4's 1923 speed record – but the Trophy and prize money were never claimed!

THE ACE LOGO
An eagle with wings spread alights on the ACE name.

Sprung saddle

Dropped handlebars were the rider's only aerodynamic aid in 1920

Contracting-band gave minimal braking | Open exhaust pipe | Tuned engine | Unsprung forks

Custom Bikes

MOTORCYCLES ARE ALMOST always modified to suit the tastes and needs of the owner. Different accessories and equipment are used by touring, sporting, and commuting riders; for example, a fairing supplies weather protection and changes the look of the motorcycle completely. Another kind of owner spends much of their time and money customizing their machines to steal the limelight at a rally, or to be the focus of attention on the street. Some will put up with personal discomfort and inconvenience for the sake of appearance – nevertheless, many extravagantly customized bikes are used daily by dedicated owners.

Custom-made leather tool roll

Beaded tassles hang from the handlebar ends

Custom design orange-and-black flame paintwork

The classic chopper look calls for high "ape-hanger" handlebars.

1951 Harley-Davidson Hydra Glide
The classic chopper is built around a Harley-Davidson engine. The basic idea evolved in the fifties and sixties when American enthusiasts started stripping their machines down to the bare essentials. The chopper look was popularized in the film "Easy Rider".

Wide rear tyre

Chromed gearbox-end cover

Braided-steel oil-delivery hose is stronger and better-looking than standard hose

Chrome
instrument
panel

1942 Indian Four

The modifications undertaken on some machines are very subtle. This 1942 Indian Four has been fitted with a pair of telescopic forks in place of its original girders. The new forks functioned better than the originals and were available as a bolt-on addition. The paint finish, and the fringed and studded leather saddle and panniers, are non-standard details.

Small Bates
headlights are
often fitted to
custom
bikes

A tassled
leather saddle
has been added

SPECIFICATIONS

1942 Indian
- **ENGINE** In-line four cylinder
- **CAPACITY** 77cu.in. (1265cc)
- **POWER OUTPUT** 35+bhp
- **TRANSMISSION** Three-speed handchange gearbox, chain drive
- **FRAME** Tubular cradle
- **SUSPENSION** Telescopic forks, sprung hub
- **WEIGHT** 568lb (258kg)
- **TOP SPEED** 90mph (145km/h)

Non-standard
passing lights

Whitewall
tyres

This machine uses standard
Harley forks taken from a
later machine. Earlier
chopper fashions
involved extending
the forks

SPECIFICATIONS

1951 Harley-Davidson Chopper
- **ENGINE** Tuned panhead overhead-valve 45° V-twin
- **CAPACITY** 94½cu.in. (1550cc)
- **POWER OUTPUT** Not assessed
- **TRANSMISSION** Four-speed gearbox, chain drive
- **FRAME** Duplex cradle
- **SUSPENSION** Rigid frame, telescopic forks
- **WEIGHT** 500lb (227kg)
- **TOP SPEED** 137mph (220km/h)

A combined oil
cooler and filter
maintains the
oil temperature
at the correct
level

Straight-leg
Hydra Glide
frame

A black finish has
been added to the
stainless steel
spokes and alloy
wheel rims

Drilled disc
brakes with
four-piston
callipers

The 1951 Panhead
engine has been enlarged
to a capacity of 94½cu. in.
(1,550cc) and fitted with
performance parts

33

Indian

Owner's record book

Indian badge

Indian matches

Gifted engineer, Oscar Hedstrom built a motorized two-wheeler in 1899. George Hendee, bicycle maker and former cycle racer, saw the potential of the machine. Together they developed a motorcycle suitable for mass production and manufacture of the "Indian" motorcycle began. From the outset quality was high and design was both sound and sophisticated. As a result competition success came quickly for Indian's factory team.

1904 Indian Single

Indian's reputation for fine quality was established with their first machine. Sound engineering was combined with the vital ruggedness needed for America's tough road conditions. It also introduced greater design sophistication such as twist-grip controls.

"Camel hump" petrol tank

Battery container

All-chain transmission

Coil for "constant loss" ignition system

A handlebar-operated advance/retard mechanism (above) controls engine speed and includes a valve-lifter for starting the motor.

SPECIFICATIONS

1904 Indian Single
- **Engine** Inlet-over-exhaust single cylinder
- **Capacity** 17.6cu in (288cc)
- **Power output** 2.5bhp
- **Transmission** Direct chain drive, no gearbox
- **Frame** Bicycle diamond-type frame with the engine as rear down tube
- **Suspension** None
- **Weight** 115lb (52kg)
- **Top speed** 30mph (48km/h)

SPECIFICATIONS

1914 Indian V-twin
- **Engine** Two-cylinder 42° V-twin
- **Capacity** 61cu. in (1000cc)
- **Power output** 7bhp
- **Transmission** Two-speed gearbox with foot and hand operation
- **Frame** Cradle
- **Suspension** Leaf-sprung front and rear forks
- **Weight** 410lb (186kg)
- **Top speed** 55mph (88km/h)

1914 Indian V-twin

Indian built their first V-twins in 1907. Oscar Hedstrom designed a "V" constructed at 42°, with cylinders and barrels similar to those of the Indian singles. The bicycle-style frame was abandoned in 1909 and swingarms and rear springing were adopted in 1913.

A passenger seat was an optional extra

Leaf sprung rear suspension

Tail light

White rubber tyres were common period fittings

Speedometer drive

Gearchange lever

Clutch lever

Silencer cut-out

Foot-pedal operates one of two rear brakes, the other is handlebar operated

- DID YOU KNOW? -
The first production motorcycle ever to be fitted with an electric starter was an Indian. The Hendee Special of 1914 was based on the standard V-twin.

Board racing events took place on banked oval tracks built of wooden planks. In the 1920s track speeds averaged over 100mph (160km/h) and horrific accidents did occur. Splinters were an inevitable hazard.

The start of a board track race.

The lead is fiercely contested.

The flag goes down on the winner.

SPECIFICATIONS

1920 Indian Boardracer
- **ENGINE** Side-valve 42° V-twin
- **CAPACITY** 60.9cu. in (998cc)
- **POWER OUTPUT** 37bhp (estimated)
- **TRANSMISSION** Direct chain drive, (no gearbox)
- **FRAME** Tubular loop frame
- **SUSPENSION** None
- **WEIGHT** 300lb (136kg) (estimated)
- **TOP SPEED** 105mph (169km/h)

1920 Indian Boardracer
A machine similar to this one, with no suspension, brakes, or gears – and based on the Indian Powerplus roadster engine but using a racing frame – achieved 99mph (159km/h) at Daytona Beach in April 1920.

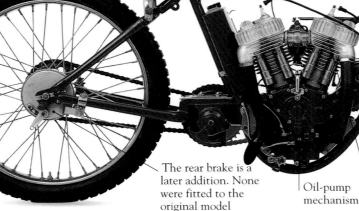

Fuel tank retaining clips

Adjustable dropped handlebars

Leather sheathed cables

The rear brake is a later addition. None were fitted to the original model

Side-valve engine

Oil-pump mechanism

Strengthening brace

1927 Indian Hillclimber
This motorcycle is a factory competition hillclimber used by Bob Armstrong, National Amateur Hillclimb Champion from 1927 to 1930.

Leather strap on ignition cutout stops the engine if the rider falls off.

SPECIFICATIONS

1927 Indian Hillclimber
- **ENGINE** Side-valve 42° V-twin
- **CAPACITY** 80cu. in (1310cc)
- **POWER OUTPUT** 39bhp (estimated)
- **TRANSMISSION** Single-speed factory competition gearbox, chain drive
- **FRAME** Open loop
- **SUSPENSION** Leaf-sprung trailing link front forks, rigid rear
- **WEIGHT** 400lb (182kg) (estimated)
- **TOP SPEED** Dependent on gearing

The fuel tank carried alcohol rather than petrol

Leaf sprung trailing-link forks

Foot clutch

Large final drive sprocket to reduce gearing

Indian Scouts & Fours

AMERICAN MOTORCYCLES NEVER challenged the supremacy of the motorcar; makers could not compete with the economic practicality of Henry Ford's mass-produced Model T. After boom years early in the century, the motorcycle market contracted rapidly and by the 1920s only three major manufacturers remained, of which Indian was the largest. When Excelsior stopped production in 1931, only Harley-Davidson and Indian were left. At that time Indians were considered to have the better design, and Harleys to be the more reliable bike; riders were fiercely loyal to their chosen brand. Indian's founders had left by 1916 and ownership changed several times. For a time, Indian was part of the group that owned the Du Pont paint company, a factor which influenced colour schemes used for the bikes.

This motorcycle tool kit was custom-made for the Indian 101 Scout shown below (main image).

Allan Ford's wall-of-death is the last example to remain active in Great Britain. He and his team of riders tour the country.

1928 Indian 101 Scout
The first Scouts, introduced in 1920, were an instant success. Launched in 1928, the 101 model, featured a longer wheelbase and lower seat height. The 101's low centre of gravity contributed to its excellent handling and made it a favourite with stunt riders, in particular with those who perform the wall-of-death. Indian decided to discontinue the 101 in 1932, and instead offered a new Scout model with the bigger, heavier chassis of the Chief (pp.38-9). The handling was inferior to that of the 101, widely regarded as the best machine Indian ever built.

The wall-of-death was invented as early as 1913. Motorcycles ridden around "the wall", a wooden drum about 30ft (10m) in diameter and 20ft (7m) high, appear to defy gravity but are actually held in place by centrifugal force. If they stop, they fall to the ground. Spectators stand at the top of the drum.

SPECIFICATIONS
1928 Indian 101 Scout
•ENGINE Side-valve 45° V-twin
•CAPACITY 37cu. in. (606cc)
•POWER OUTPUT 18bhp (estimated)
•TRANSMISSION Three-speed hand-change gearbox, chain drive
•FRAME Tubular steel cradle
•SUSPENSION Leaf-sprung trailing link forks, rigid rear
•WEIGHT 370lb (168kg)
•TOP SPEED 75mph (121km/h)

English-style bars

Auxiliary hand pump increases oil feed during hard use

Gearchange lever

Valve lifter

Embossed leaf-sprung kickstarter pedal

Front brakes fitted from 1928

The Indian Fours

In 1927 Indian obtained the rights to the ACE motorcycle (p.31), adding a four-cylinder machine to their range. Cleveland and Henderson had ceased production in 1931, but Indian persevered with fours until 1943. Fours were expensive to build and investment in them, rather than V-twins, contributed to Indian's demise.

SPECIFICATIONS

1939 Indian 439

- **ENGINE** In-line, inlet-over-exhaust, four cylinder
- **CAPACITY** 77cu. in. (1265cc)
- **POWER OUTPUT** 40bhp (estimated)
- **TRANSMISSION** Three-speed gearbox, chain drive
- **FRAME** Tubular steel cradle
- **SUSPENSION** Leaf-sprung trailing-link forks, rigid rear
- **WEIGHT** 532lb (241kg)
- **TOP SPEED** 90mph (145km/h)

Tyre pump

Messinger leather saddle

Panel light

Rocker cover

Speedometer drive

Exhaust heat-shield

Double down-tube frame replaced the ACE single down-tube version

Oil-pressure gauge

Comple valve gear enclosure

Streamline mudguards

SPECIFICATIONS

1930 Indian 402

- **ENGINE** In-line inlet-over-exhaust four cylinder
- **CAPACITY** 77cu. in. (1265cc)
- **POWER OUTPUT** 30bhp
- **TRANSMISSION** Three-speed handchange gearbox, chain drive
- **FRAME** Tubular steel cradle
- **SUSPENSION** Leaf-sprung trailing-link forks, rigid rear
- **WEIGHT** 455lb (207kg)
- **TOP SPEED** 75mph (121km/h)

SPECIFICATIONS

1948 Indian 648 Scout

- **ENGINE** Side-valve 42° V-twin
- **CAPACITY** 46cu. in (737cc)
- **POWER OUTPUT** 38bhp
- **TRANSMISSION** Four-speed handchange gearbox, chain drive
- **FRAME** Tubular steel cradle
- **SUSPENSION** Girder forks, rigid rear
- **WEIGHT** 400lb (182kg) (estimated)
- **TOP SPEED** 115mph (185km/h)

Trailing-link leaf-sprung forks were first used in 1910

The chrome rims fitted to this motorcycle are a later non-standard addition

1948 Daytona race programme

1948 Indian 648 Scout

The last Scouts were built in 1948 to uphold Indian's name in racing. Only fifty 648 Scouts were built; this machine was ridden to victory by Floyd Emde in the 1948 Daytona 200-mile race.

Floyd Emde, 1948 Daytona race winner

Girder forks with friction dampers

Magneto

Indian Chief oil pump

Indian Chief

INDIAN'S HEYDAY CAME before the First World War, but the
Chief, designed by Charles Franklin, made its debut later, in
1922. Advanced design allowed the Chief, together with its
famous stablemate the Scout (pp.36-7), to dominate the market
place for over twenty years. However, Indian management was
less efficient than their motorcycles and, despite the quality of the
product, the marque declined. Improvements were made to the
design, but by the 1950s the bike was outdated compared with
Harleys of the period. Ralph Rogers bought the company and
invested heavily in new designs but his attempt to rescue
Indian ended in disaster. The new models were expensive
to build and proved unreliable. Later Indian's name
was attached to imported bikes and the firm declined
further. The Chiefs were the last true Indians.

The fastest ever Indian achieved a speed
of 190mph (306km/h) at the Bonneville Salt
Flats in 1960. The machine was a 1920 Scout,
extensively modified by New Zealander
Burt Munroe.

1947 Indian Chief
*Colour options, tank, mudguards, and tyres for
the Chief varied throughout its long production
run. The later Chiefs (such as this fine example)
were particularly handsome machines. Valanced
mudguards (or "fenders") and girder forks gave
the 1947 model a look of elegance and
streamlined luxury, although its
performance was rather sluggish –
because of its weight – and its
speed and acceleration
could not match the
equivalent Harley-
Davidson.*

Skirted fenders were
introduced in 1940

Luxurious sprung leather
saddle, with chrome-plated
grab-rail for the passenger

Balloon tyres greatly
increase the comfort
of the ride, but do
entail a sacrifice in
handling quality

The rear wheel is mounted on
a plunger rear suspension unit

Rear brake
linkage

Indian's "own brand" engine oils, like Harley-Davidson's (p.163), were manufactured to their own specification by petroleum companies.

Viewed from above, the hand gearchange lever, cap for main petrol tank, and instruments are seen to be beautifully designed.

The right-hand twist-grip controls the ignition timing, not the throttle. (Indian practice since 1901)

Caps for oil tank and reserve fuel tank

Chromed headlight and additional sidelights

Illuminated Indian mascot

Girder forks replaced the traditional leaf-sprung design

Gearchange linkage (The lever is on the other side)

The small drum-brake is barely sufficient to stop a 550lb (249kg) motorcycle

Other Classics

1910 Yale

Yale machines were produced at Toledo, Ohio, from 1902 until 1915. Two models were produced, a 6½ horse-power V-twin, and the single cylinder machine shown here. The company became well known in America particularly for its big 950cc V-twin, equipped with a two-speed gearbox and chain drive to the rear wheel.

The handlebar-mounted, twist-grip throttle control, has twelve separate rods and linkages to connect it to the carburettor.

SPECIFICATIONS
1912 Yale
- **ENGINE** Inlet-over-exhaust single cylinder
- **CAPACITY** 39½cu. in (649cc)
- **POWER OUTPUT** 3½bhp
- **TRANSMISSION** Single speed, belt drive
- **FRAME** Tubular diamond frame with engine as stressed member
- **SUSPENSION** Sagger spring forks, rigid rear
- **WEIGHT** 160lb (72.6kg)
- **TOP SPEED** 45mph (72km/h)

Flexible-ended twist grips reduce road shock to the rider

Oil is stored in the rear of petrol tank

Endless belt final drive. Removable frame sections allow for replacement

Acetylene lighting

Skip-tooth chain wheel

Cast alloy engine has a crankcase window to inspect the oil level

The leading link fork was produced by the Sagger company and sold to many manufacturers of the period

1929 Cleveland Tornado

The Cleveland company began producing lightweight motorcycles in 1915. It entered the four-cylinder market in 1925. Although its design followed the style established by the Henderson, the Cleveland's smaller capacity model left it at a performance disadvantage compared to the opposition. In 1929, the basic machine was improved to produce "The Tornado". Careful tuning gave increased power yet, despite the undoubted quality of their product, Cleveland closed down in 1929.

The back of the Cleveland

Frame design gives a low seat height.

SPECIFICATIONS
1929 Cleveland Tornado
- **ENGINE** In-line, inlet-over-exhaust four cylinder
- **CAPACITY** 61cu. in (1000cc)
- **POWER OUTPUT** 31bhp (estimated)
- **TRANSMISSION** Three-speed handchange gearbox, chain drive
- **FRAME** Tubular steel cradle
- **SUSPENSION** Leading axle forks, rigid rear
- **WEIGHT** 540lb (245kg)
- **TOP SPEED** 100mph (160km/h)

"Drop centre" rims use beaded-edge tyres

The Cleveland was one of the earliest American machines to be equipped with a front brake

The crankcase is horizontally split on this large, wet sump engine

1920 Excelsior 20R/1930 Excelsior Super X

Excelsior motorcycles were built in Chicago by the Schwinn company, which, from 1917, also made Hendersons. Production of the Excelsior began in 1907 and was abruptly halted in 1931 with the onset of the depression. During that time they established themselves as the smaller of the "Big Three" manufacturers after Indian and Harley-Davidson. An Excelsior was the first machine ever to be timed at over 100mph (160km/h) in 1913. These high-performance machines won many races. The Super X, Excelsior's most famous model, was introduced in 1925 and was the first American 45 cubic inch motorcycle; Indian and Harley-Davidson followed suit.

The V-twin engine has iron barrels and painted alloy cases.

Throttle cable linkage

The seat post infringed Harley-Davidson patents and was abandoned

A silencer bypass, fitted to improve performance

A detachable frame rail permits engine removal

A puncture caused the tyre to leave Clincher rims. They were abandoned by the mid twenties

SPECIFICATIONS
1920 Excelsior 20R
- **ENGINE** Inlet-over-exhaust 45° V-twin
- **CAPACITY** 61cu. in (1000cc)
- **POWER OUTPUT** 20bhp
- **TRANSMISSION** Three-speed handchange gearbox, chain drive
- **FRAME** Tubular steel cradle with stressed engine
- **SUSPENSION** Trailing link forks
- **WEIGHT** 500lb (227kg) (estimated)
- **TOP SPEED** 100mph (160 km/h)

SPECIFICATIONS
1930 Excelsior Super X
- **ENGINE** Inlet-over-exhaust 45° V-twin
- **CAPACITY** 45.5cu. in (746cc)
- **POWER OUTPUT** 20bhp (estimated)
- **TRANSMISSION** Three-speed handchange gearbox, chain drive
- **FRAME** Tubular steel frame with engine as stressed member
- **SUSPENSION** Leading link forks, rigid rear
- **WEIGHT** 450lb (204kg) (estimated)
- **TOP SPEED** 65mph (105km/h)

The fuel supply is on the right of the tank, the oil and reserve petrol on the left. The factory named the bike's styling the Streamline

The Messinger sprung saddle

Klaxon horn

The clutch mechanism has no return spring, and can be left disengaged.

The valve lifter is operated by the first quarter turn of the kick start

Germany

*Although known as the birthplace of the motorcycle, Germany now
has only one major production company – BMW.*

Gottlieb Daimler developed the first gasoline-powered
motorcycle in 1885 (pp.8-9), but he soon turned to three-
and four-wheeled vehicles. Hildebrand and Wolfmüller
(p.11) began producing four-cylinder
motorcycles in Munich in 1894; they
made the world's first commercially
built motorbikes. The Hildebrand
and Wolfmüller survived for three
years, until the design was made
obsolete by the development of the
De Dion engine in France. The
availability of these engines, and
similar units from firms like Zedel,
made it possible for many European
bicycle manufacturers to turn to
motorcycle production. In
Germany, bicycle makers
including NSU and Adler began producing
motorcycle frames at the turn of the
century; NSU started building their
own engines too. Adler stopped
making motorbikes in 1909; they
came back in 1949 with a series of
advanced two-stroke machines, but disappeared in 1958. Fafnir also first built
engines before building complete bikes.

MZ Trophy petrol cap

A Growing Industry
In the aftermath of
the First World War,
the Allies imposed
severe restrictions upon
the production output of
the German armaments
industry. Zündapp (p.60)
had built artillery guns
during the conflict, while
BMW built aircraft engines.
Both turned to motorcycle
production: Zündapp built
their first bike in 1921 and the

*Rear mudguard of
Horex Imperator*

*Front view
of BMW
Kompressor*

first BMW (p.45), a flat twin with shaft drive, appeared two
years later. Many other small German companies sprang up
in the post-war years, yet all but the strongest disappeared in
the economic decline of the late twenties. DKW, (pp.48-9)
founded in 1921, grew so quickly that within ten years they
were the world's biggest motorcycle manufacturer. The new
political regime wanted German machines to succeed on the
race tracks of the world and made a substantial amount of
money available for the development of advanced racing
machinery. BMW, DKW, and NSU all enjoyed competition

success in this period, with their
supercharged racing machines that
left the opposition struggling.

Münch Mammoth logo

East and West Germany
When, in 1945, Germany was split
in two, the Eastern zone housed the
DKW factory. DKW was renamed
IFA when production resumed in
1945, and many of the key staff fled
to the West, taking the DKW name
with them. For years there were
similarities between the two makes.
IFA became MZ (pp.52-3) in the late fifties: MZ took two-
stroke prizes, as DKW had done, and are largely
responsible for the development of the modern
two-stroke, though the company never had
the funds to capitalize on its expertise.
Other East German factories, EMW,
AWO, and Simpson, produced
copies of the pre-war BMW shaft-
driven, single-cylinder machines.

A Fluctuating Market
In the West, the post-war chaos created a
demand for cheap two-wheelers that was
satisfied by the production of mopeds and
scooters by existing firms such as DKW,
Zündapp, and NSU, as well as newcomers
such as the aircraft company Heinkel
(p.99), whose production skills were applied
to making scooters. Once the post-war boom
was over, the market contracted sharply. Many
firms were taken by surprise: TWN, Adler, and
Horex all stopped production of motorcycles in
1958. BMW proceeded from
crisis to crisis in the post-war
period, before becoming
stable in the mid-sixties.
German domestic prosperity
in the sixties and seventies
reduced demand for motorcycles:
more people could afford cars and
motorcycle makers suffered again.
NSU stopped building motorcycles in the sixties. DKW
stopped as well. Hercules
and Zündapp lasted into the
seventies. BMW are now the
only significant survivors of a
once massive industry.

*Back view
of BMW
Rennsport*

BMW

U NTIL THE FIRST WORLD WAR, BMW built only aircraft engines. In 1921, they built a horizontally opposed twin-cylinder motorcycle engine for a number of German manufacturers, including Victoria (p.60). In 1923, BMW unveiled a complete motorcycle by aircraft designer Max Friz: a 500cc engine was fitted into the frame with the crankshaft running lengthways and the cylinders protruding sideways. Its simple, effective layout is still used.

The first BMW motorcycle established design trends that the company still follow today. An integral gearbox was among its advanced features.

1935 BMW R12

The R12 was popular for sidecar and solo purposes. It was the first production machine to use a four-speed gearbox and hydraulically damped telescopic forks: a feature pioneered by BMW. They abandoned telescopic forks in the late forties and adopted Earles forks.

A pillion saddle bolts onto the luggage rack

Gearchange lever

Pressed-steel frame

Hydraulically damped telescopic forks

Four-speed gearbox

Footboard

Exposed drive shaft

SPECIFICATIONS

1935 BMW R12

- •ENGINE Horizontally opposed side-valve twin
- •CAPACITY 745cc
- •POWER OUTPUT 20bhp @ 4,000rpm
- •TRANSMISSION Four-speed gearbox, shaft drive
- •FRAME Pressed-steel cradle frame
- •SUSPENSION Telescopic forks
- •WEIGHT 188kg (414lb)
- •TOP SPEED 120km/h (75mph)

1939 BMW Kompressor

In 1936 BMW adopted an overhead camshaft for each cylinder for competition machines. A version with a full fairing broke the land speed record, and also competed superbly in international races. Georg Meier won the 1938 European Championships and the 1939 Senior TT (below). His team mate Jock West was second.

Georg Meier on the way to winning the 1939 Isle of Man Senior TT.

Adjustable suspension damper

Plug spanner and spare plugs

Leather-covered chin pad

Tapered section tubing makes the frame stronger

Inlet manifold (running from the supercharger)

The supercharger pressurizes the fuel mixture

1954 BMW Rennsport

For the 1953 race season, BMW built a new overhead-camshaft 500cc based on the pre-war design. The following year they built the first small batch of Rennsports for private racers. They were raced throughout the 1950s but never realized their promise as solo machines. In the sidecar class, Rennsports were dominant from 1954 to 1973, and BMW always won the manufacturers' title.

Walter Schneider and passenger Hans Strauss were world champions in 1958 and 1959 in the Rennsport outfit.

Air cooling is excellent but the exposed cylinders risk crash damage.

Earles forks were stronger than telescopics and ideal for sidecar events

Twin leading-shoe drum brake

Oil sump

The magneto is gear driven from the front of the engine

Dell'Orto carburettors

Clutch actuating arm

Tapered megaphone exhaust

Mesh screen

Linked brakes can be operated by handlebar lever or foot pedal

Single carburettor protected by aluminium cowling

Shaft drive to overhead cams

SPECIFICATIONS

1954 BMW Rennsport

- •ENGINE Horizontally opposed four-stroke twin, bevel driven overhead camshaft
- •CAPACITY 494cc
- •POWER OUTPUT 48bhp @ 8,000rpm
- •TRANSMISSION Four-speed gearbox, shaft drive
- •FRAME Twin loop with single top tube
- •SUSPENSION Earles-type pivoted forks, rear swingarm
- •WEIGHT 136kg (300lb)
- •TOP SPEED 201km/h (125mph)

SPECIFICATIONS

1939 Kompressor Type 255

- •ENGINE Double overhead-camshaft flat twin
- •CAPACITY 492cc
- •POWER OUTPUT 55bhp @ 7000rpm (estimated)
- •TRANSMISSION Four-speed, shaft drive
- •FRAME Tubular steel cradle
- •SUSPENSION Telescopic forks, rear plunger units
- •WEIGHT 137kg (302lb)
- •TOP SPEED 210km/h (130mph)

BMW's advertisements celebrate their success in taking the motorcycle speed record on six occasions during the thirties, finally pushing the record up to 279.5km/h (173.6mph) in 1937.

The Later BMWs

BMW ROAD MACHINES were always expensive, well-constructed bikes. However in the late sixties, the company took on Italian, Japanese, and British makers by offering more up-to-date machines. Production costs were reduced and the price of the bikes was lowered. A range of new, high-performance models with four cylinders and water cooling appeared in 1983, but public demand kept the classic twin-cylinder in production.

SPECIFICATIONS
1961 BMW R69/S
- **ENGINE** Horizontally opposed overhead-valve flat twin
- **CAPACITY** 594cc
- **POWER OUTPUT** 42bhp
- **TRANSMISSION** Four-speed gearbox, shaft drive
- **FRAME** Tubular steel cradle frame
- **SUSPENSION** Earles forks, rear swingarm
- **WEIGHT** 202kg (445lb)
- **TOP SPEED** 177km/h (110mph)

1961 BMW R69/S
Based on the more sedate R69 of 1955, the R69/S was the last of the old-style BMWs. Very little was changed during its production run between 1959 and 1969. A 500cc version was also built.

The Hoske 30 litre (6½ gallon) fuel tank was not standard

Air filter

Leading-link Earles forks were used on BMW road bikes from 1955 to 1969

The gearbox action is notoriously clunky partly due to the engine-speed clutch

The kickstart pivots away from the bike

Ignition key and light switch

Speedometer

Good functional design, such as this clear instrument panel, typifies the BMW look.

THE BMW SINGLES

In addition to their famous flat twins, BMW produced single-cylinder motor-cycles by mounting one cylinder of a twin vertically. Shaft drive was used as usual. Production of singles ceased in 1967. This model is a 1957 R26.

Tubular steel cradle frame

Pagusa saddle

Tank-top tool box

Leading-link forks

Non-standard British-made panniers

Single-cylinder engine

1975 BMW R90/S

With the 90/S BMW shed their staid image and black livery to produce a fast and fashionable machine. The claimed top speed of 200km/h (124mph) matched any Italian or Japanese rival, but the BMW cost twice as much.

A bikini fairing conceals instruments, clock, and voltmeter

Cowlings hide starter motor and air cleaner

Fogged paintwork means that no two R90/Ss are identical

Horizontal cylinders have become BMW's trademark

Drilled discs were supposed to improve wet weather braking

Dell'Orto accelerator pump carburettors

Heat from the cylinder discolours the single-skin exhaust

SPECIFICATIONS
1992 BMW K1
- **ENGINE** In-line four cylinder double-overhead-camshaft
- **CAPACITY** 988cc
- **POWER OUTPUT** 100 bhp
- **TRANSMISSION** Five- speed, shaft drive
- **FRAME** Tubular lattice frame
- **SUSPENSION** Telescopic forks, rear swingarm
- **WEIGHT** 258kg (569lb)
- **TOP SPEED** 238km/h (148mph)

1992 BMW K1

Following the introduction of four-cylinder machines, a new flagship BMW was unveiled in 1989. The sixteen-valve cylinder head supplied increased power to the K1. Anti-lock brakes were an option.

SPECIFICATIONS
1975 BMW R90/S
- **ENGINE** Overhead-valve flat twin
- **CAPACITY** 898cc
- **POWER OUTPUT** 67bhp @ 7,000rpm
- **TRANSMISSION** Five-speed, shaft drive
- **FRAME** Tubular steel cradle frame
- **SUSPENSION** Telescopic forks, rear swingarm
- **WEIGHT** 215kg (474lb)
- **TOP SPEED** 201km/h (125mph)

A single-sided rear swingarm was used on all BMW machines by the end of the 1980s.

The removable seat hump conceals a pillion seat

Storage compartments

Aerodynamic fairing designed in a wind tunnel

Anti-lock braking trigger

Fuel-injected sixteen-valve engine

Stainless steel exhaust system

DKW

DKW WAS FOUNDED IN 1919 in Zschoppau by an expatriate Dane, Skafte Rasmussen. Beginning with a simple motor attached to a bicycle, they produced reliable, well-designed, two-stroke machines. By the 1930s DKW were the world's largest motorcycle manufacturer and racing experience gave them the lead in two-stroke technology.

Their very effective split-single designs won the European Championship four times before the war. The 1950s saw sales decline; DKW finally closed in the 1960s.

1937 DKW SS250

This supercharged split-single had three pistons but only one combustion chamber. The horizontal front cylinder, acted as a supercharger, forcing the charge through the transfer port under pressure, and into the combustion chamber. The transfer port is controlled by the first vertical piston, while the exhaust port is controlled by the rear piston, allowing for more extreme port timing.

Ewald Kluge was the top DKW rider in pre-war years. He won the European Championship in 1938 and 1939.

SPECIFICATIONS

DKW SS250

- **ENGINE** Water-cooled split-single two-stroke with supercharger
- **BORE AND STROKE** Not available
- **CAPACITY** 250cc
- **POWER OUTPUT** 25bhp
- **CARBURATION** Twin carburettors with automatic reed valve
- **IGNITION** Magneto
- **TRANSMISSION** Four-speed gearbox, chain drive
- **CLUTCH** Wet multiplate
- **FRAME** Tubular cradle
- **SUSPENSION** Girder forks, plunger with swingarm
- **BRAKES** Drum brakes, front and rear
- **WEIGHT** 95kg (210lb)
- **TOP SPEED** 185km/h (115mph)
- **YEAR OF CONSTRUCTION** 1937

The DKW racers used so much petrol that a huge fuel tank was essential

The tuned megaphone exhausts of a DKW could be heard 13km (8 miles) away from races

Rear suspension is achieved by a combination of plunger springing and swingarm

Rear torque-arm, drilled to reduce weight

Twin carburettors mounted on each side of the engine

DKW works racers evolved quickly. This 250cc version, photographed at the 1938 T.T. races, is equipped with forward-mounted carburettors and a supercharger.

DKW AND THE HARLEY-DAVIDSON 125

During the Second World War DKW built a versatile machine called the RT 125. When production restarted this was the first model to be re-introduced. The design was so good that other makers around the world copied it freely when the design was handed over as part of Germany's war reparations. Harley's 125, BSA's Bantam, and the first Yamaha, were all derived from the DKW.

Sprung saddle (no rear suspension)

Teleglide forks

125cc four-port engine inspired by DKW

Five-inch (12.7cm) drum brake

The four ring motif of the Auto Union is still used by Audi today

DKW's famous name needed little advertising. Most of Germany's greatest riders belonged to their international race team. When DKW became part of the Zweirad Union, their name was used in export markets.

Girder forks

Water-cooling radiator

The DKW's split single engine has two pistons and cylinders but only one combustion chamber

Alloy wheel rims to reduce weight

Air-scoop to cool the drum-brake. If they overheat, drum brakes tend to lose efficiency, or fade out

The engine uses a horizontal Ladepumpe supercharging cylinder

Sidecars

German Steib sidecars were renowned for their quality. BMW and Zündapp buyers could order their new bike with a Steib attached.

M OTORCYCLING families have benefited from the increased carrying-capacity of sidecars – a factor that far outweighs increased fuel consumption and loss of manoeuvrability. Riding a combination is completely unlike riding a solo machine: the handlebars must be physically pulled to change direction. The sidecar tries to overtake the bike when braking; however slight acceleration will cause the reverse to occur.

In the 1920s, a motorcycle and sidecar provided ideal family transport. Cheap cars ended the popularity of the sidecar.

Side light

Links vary the angle between chair and bike

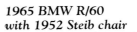

1965 BMW R/60 with 1952 Steib chair
Fitting a sidecar changes the stresses imposed upon the chassis of the bike. The forks receive especially heavy treatment. The Earles forks used by BMW from 1955 to 1969 are ideal for sidecar use and were a reason for the popularity of BMWs with enthusiasts.

Setting up the bike and chair is a subtle process. To achieve neutral handling, the bike must lean away marginally from the chair, and the sidecar wheel must point inwards slightly. The position of the sidecar wheel, relative to the wheelbase of the bike, also affects handling.

Sidecar sidelight

SPECIFICATIONS

1965 BMW R/60
- •ENGINE Horizontally opposed overhead-valve, four-stroke air-cooled twin
- •CAPACITY 594cc
- •POWER OUTPUT 28bhp
- •TRANSMISSION Four-speed, shaft drive
- •FRAME Tubular cradle
- •SUSPENSION Earles forks, rear swingarm
- •WEIGHT 202kg (445lb) plus 68kg (150lb) for the sidecar
- •TOP SPEED 120km/h (75mph)

Lockable luggage boot

Knock-off wheel nuts

The wheel of the sidecar is rubber-sprung

The frame rail around the sidecar doubles as a bumper bar

SPECIFICATIONS

1923 Douglas

- **ENGINE** Cast-iron, air-cooled flat twin
- **CAPACITY** 497cc
- **POWER OUTPUT** Not known
- **TRANSMISSION** Three-speed hand-change gearbox, chain-drive
- **FRAME** Tubular cradle with and hinged Dixon racing sidecar
- **SUSPENSION** Girder forks, rigid rear
- **WEIGHT** 200lb (91kg) (est)
- **TOP SPEED** 104km/h (64mph) (est)

1923 Douglas and Dixon Banking Sidecar

Sidecar classes began to appear in many motorcycle events from 1920 onwards (pp.166-70). The banking sidecar shown with the Douglas was designed by Freddie Dixon. Its wheel axle could be raised or lowered by the passenger to give the correct angle of inclination of the machine and achieve the best possible cornering speeds.

Sidecar control lever

A front view of the Douglas and sidecar clearly shows the vital control levers.

8717MN

The bike's gearing must be lowered to pull the sidecar

Freddie Dixon won the 1923 sidecar TT driving a banking sidecar similar to the one shown above. His passenger was Walter Perry.

The classic Steib bullet-shaped sidecar was built until the 1960s

A motorcycle and sidecar, being used to carry six people, climbs a hill in Sevenoaks, Kent, England.

SPORTS SIDECARS

Sidecar technology has changed little over the years. If the sidecar is to be removable, complicated braking and steering systems are precluded. This 1923 Douglas uses a banking sidecar; the angle of lean is controlled by a lever which is operated by the passenger.

For left-hand corners the sidecar wheel is dropped.

For right-hand corners, the sidecar wheel is raised.

MZ

W̲HEN G̲ERMANY DIVIDED after the Second World War, the Zschopau factory, formerly DKW (pp.48-9), was in the East. Many of the personnel relocated in the West, taking the name with them. Production restarted at Zschopau which became known as MZ – Motorradwerke Zschopau – building machines based on DKW designs. Production MZs were often rugged, utilitarian machines, but racers, developed by Walter Kaaden, led two-stroke technology in the sixties.

Ernst Degner defected to Suzuki in 1961, taking MZ's secrets with him.

1965 MZ RE125

MZ's 125cc was the first engine to achieve a power output of 200 bhp per litre, (at the time, 100bhp per litre was considered to be excellent). By 1965 MZ's advantage, and Grand Prix victories, were diminishing. Teams with better funding took their ideas and developed them using better materials.

Water-temperature gauge

Water-temperature sensor

Radiator

Cylinder water jacket

Rev counter drive from end of crankshaft

Dry clutch

Rear-facing exhaust ports with spring clips to exhaust

Double-sided brake

Gear-driven magneto

Carburettor feeds crankcase via disc valve

The MZ's scientifically designed exhaust creates a natural supercharging effect by using pressure waves from the spent charge to increase the crankcase pressure.

SPECIFICATIONS

1965 MZ RE125

- •ENGINE Single-cylinder water-cooled two stroke
- •CAPACITY 124cc
- •POWER OUTPUT 25bhp (estimated)
- •TRANSMISSION Eight-speed gearbox, chain drive
- •FRAME Tubular steel cradle
- •SUSPENSION Telescopic forks, rear swingarm
- •WEIGHT 91kg (200lb)
- •TOP SPEED 210km/h (131mph)

1973 MZ Trophy ES250/2

The Trophy was an ungainly motor-cycle capable of excellent perform-ance. Its long exhaust pipe, bizarre front forks, and generally eccentric styling were replaced in the mid-seventies by a rather more conventional-looking machine that housed the same power unit.

A heat shield protects the rider from the expansion chamber exhausts

Side panels hide air filter and electrics

Curious styling became a famous MZ trademark

Cast-in levers for suspension adjustment

Earles forks

40cm (16in) wheels

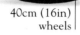

The petrol cap records MZ's International Six Days Trials successes.

A balancing weight attached to the wheel rim improves stability

SPECIFICATIONS

1973 MZ Trophy ES250/2
- ENGINE Single-cylinder two stroke
- CAPACITY 243cc
- POWER OUTPUT 17.5bhp
- TRANSMISSION Four-speed gearbox, chain drive
- FRAME Tubular steel cradle
- SUSPENSION Earles forks, rear swingarm
- WEIGHT 156kg (344lb)
- TOP SPEED 116km/h (72mph)

1985 MZ ISDT

Although World Championship success in the Grand Prix eluded them, MZ had considerable success in off-road competition. Their bikes were widely used for cross-country events, particularly in the International Six Days Trial (now known as the International Six Days Enduro (p.155)). Specialized machines were used by East German and other teams to win many medals in this gruelling sport.

Wide handlebars improve control of the bike

Flexible mudguards

Speedometer mounted on fork

Enclosed chain

The five-port engine is based on the road bike

The twin shock absorbers are mounted near swingarm pivot for increased suspension travel

SPECIFICATIONS

1985 MZ 1SDT
- ENGINE Two stroke
- CAPACITY 250cc
- POWER OUTPUT 38bhp
- TRANSMISSION Four-speed gearbox, chain drive
- FRAME Tubular cradle
- SUSPENSION Telescopic forks, rear swingarm with inboard shock absorbers
- WEIGHT 113kg (250lb)
- TOP SPEED 145km/h (90mph)

Münch

FRIEDL MÜNCH WAS associated with the Horex marque (p.61) until its demise in 1959. He then started up his own business supplying specialist components for motorcycles, especially brakes. In the mid-sixties Münch was given a commission to build a high-performance motorcycle. He used as its basis an engine taken from an NSU car, the result was the Münch Mammoth. The four-cylinder engine gave the machine a 200km/h (125mph) top speed; it cruised at over 180km/h (110mph). Münch produced many prototypes and racing machines, but the Mammoth is his most famous motorcycle – it was simply the fastest, most powerful, most expensive bike of its time.

Tacho drive from camshaft

Camshaft drive-chain cover

Clutch cover

The massive proportions of the Münch Mammoth's frame, front forks, fuel tank, and powerful twin headlights are clear in this front shot of the bike.

1967 Münch Mammoth 4TTS
When launched, the vast, hand-built Münch, named the "Mammoth", afforded levels of comfort and performance previously unknown. Limited production began in 1966. The highly appropriate name had to be dropped for copy-right reasons.

Cast alloy rear mudguard, seat with integral shock absorber mountings

Webber twin-choke carburettors

Breather pipe

Elektron-cast alloy rear wheels were adopted because early machines were so powerful that they destroyed spoked wheels

Starter-motor solenoid switch. There is no kickstarter

MÜNCH 4 1200

The Münch badge boasts of its huge power potential.

When the first 996cc Mammoth was built, twin-cylinder 750cc bikes were considered big. The massive four-cylinder Münch was sensational. Later versions increased the capacity of the NSU engine, and some versions had fuel-injection.

Lifting handle for centre-stand

Camshaft drive chain cover

An ignition lock is mounted on the side cover

Fully-enclosed chain

Handlebar-end mirror

Large capacity fuel tank

Twin-headlight nacelle with speedometer and rev counter

Rocker cover retaining springs

The legs of the forks are protected by rubber gaiters

Airscoop helps to keep the drum-brake cool and efficient

Two-piece primary drive casing

The finned sump helps to keep the oil cool

Alloy wheel rims are used for lighter weight

SPECIFICATIONS

Münch Mammoth 4TTS
- **ENGINE** Overhead-camshaft, in-line four cylinder
- **BORE AND STROKE** 75 x 66.6mm
- **CAPACITY** 1177cc
- **POWER OUTPUT** 88bhp @ 6,000rpm
- **CARBURATION** Two twin-choke Webber carburettors
- **IGNITION** Battery and coil
- **TRANSMISSION** Four-speed gearbox, chain drive
- **CLUTCH** Wet multiplate
- **FRAME** Tubular steel cradle
- **SUSPENSION** Telescopic forks, rear swingarm
- **BRAKES** Drum brakes front and rear
- **WEIGHT** 298kg (656lb)
- **TOP SPEED** 220km/h (137mph)
- **YEAR OF CONSTRUCTION** 1967

NSU

THE INITIALS NSU stand for Neckarsulm Strickmaschinen Union because, although it soon branched out into bicycle production, the company originally produced knitting machines. NSU went on to build motorcycles in 1901. Only a few makers, including Daimler (p.8-9), Hildebrand and Wolfmuller (p.10), and Victoria (p.60), preceded them. NSU built and exported a range of designs worldwide; high-quality construction enabled them to thrive until the 1960s.

SPECIFICATIONS
1901 NSU
- **ENGINE** Inlet-over-exhaust, single cylinder
- **CAPACITY** 234cc
- **POWER OUTPUT** 1.75hp
- **TRANSMISSION** Single speed, chain drive
- **FRAME** Bicycle frame with clamp-on Zedel engine
- **SUSPENSION** None
- **WEIGHT** 40kg (95lb)
- **TOP SPEED** 48km/h (30mph)

1901 NSU
Bicycle makers NSU followed the usual path into motorcycle manufacture by bolting a Swiss 1.5hp Zedel engine on to a standard bicycle frame. NSU began production in 1901, and built their own single cylinder and V-twin engines in 1903.

Early NSU motorcycles carried the full name Neckarsulm – the town where they were made – as their trade mark.

Contracting-band front brake

NSU's advertising promised superb design and construction.

SPECIFICATIONS
1931 NSU 500SS
- **ENGINE** Overhead-camshaft single
- **CAPACITY** 494cc
- **POWER OUTPUT** 22bhp @ 4,400rpm
- **TRANSMISSION** Four-speed gearbox, chain drive
- **FRAME** Tubular cradle
- **SUSPENSION** Girder forks
- **WEIGHT** 165kg (364lb)
- **TOP SPEED** 130km/h (92mph)

1931 NSU 500SS
In 1929, leading British designer Walter Moore left Norton, where he had created the overhead camshaft CS1, the first of a great line of Norton singles, and joined NSU. His first NSU designs, such as this 500SS, bore an uncanny resemblance to the Nortons and won many races.

Girder forks

Drive housing for overhead camshaft

1957 NSU Supermax

The NSU Max was originally introduced in 1952 with a number of innovative design features: pressed steel frame, leading link forks, and an overhead-camshaft engine. Twin rear shock absorbers were added when it became the Supermax in 1955. The final Supermax derivative ceased production in 1963, due to expanded NSU car production.

Period advertising extols the virtues of the Supermax, one of the most advanced machines of its day.

The NSU marque

SPECIFICATIONS

1957 NSU Supermax
- **ENGINE** Overhead-camshaft single cylinder
- **CAPACITY** 247cc
- **POWER OUTPUT** 18bhp @ 6,500rpm
- **TRANSMISSION** Four-speed gearbox, chain drive
- **FRAME** Pressed steel spine
- **SUSPENSION** Leading link forks, rear swingarm
- **WEIGHT** 174kg (383lb)
- **TOP SPEED** 120km/h (75mph)

A sprung saddle increases the rider's comfort

Leading link forks

The engine hangs from a pressed steel frame

Snail-cam chain-adjusters

The speedometer is driven from the front wheel hub

Dustbin fairings, as seen on the Sportmax left and below, were banned from race bikes in 1958.

Air scoops for cooling engine

1954 NSU Sportmax

In 1953 and '54 NSU won the 250cc World Championship with their Rennmax racing machines after which the factory withdrew from competition. They continued to sell Sportmax racers based on their 250cc road bikes. Herman-Peter Müller became World Champion in 1955 riding a Sportmax.

SPECIFICATIONS

1954 NSU Sportmax
- **ENGINE** Overhead-camshaft single cylinder
- **CAPACITY** 247cc
- **POWER OUTPUT** 28bhp @ 9,000rpm
- **TRANSMISSION** Four-speed gearbox, chain drive
- **FRAME** Pressed steel spine
- **SUSPENSION** Leading link forks, rear swingarm
- **WEIGHT** 112kg (246lb)
- **TOP SPEED** 201km/h (125mph)

Ventilated front brake hub

The engine is a tuned version of the road-going Max

Oil is carried in the frame

NSU Rennmax

NSU BUILT RACING MACHINES for the first time in 1905, and took part in the TT races (pp.152-3) as early as 1907. In the 1930s NSU raced a series of successful supercharged bikes, but the post-war ban on supercharging in international races prompted the design of new bikes. A short-lived, unsuccessful, 500cc four-cylinder appeared in 1951, followed by a 125cc single, the Rennfox, and a 250cc twin, the Rennmax, based on the experimental four. The two new bikes won their respective championships before the factory withdrew from racing in 1954.

Werner Haas, part of NSU's world-beating team, and the legendary Rennmax.

1953 NSU Rennmax
The original 1952 Rennmax used a conventional tubular frame, then, in 1953, a new pressed-steel chassis, similar to that used on Max roadsters, was introduced. In 1954, the design was updated again with a six-speed gearbox and improved camshaft drive.

A chest pad made of leather extends from the saddle

Elbow pads

Triangulated supports for shock-absorber mountings

Fuel tap

Battery holder (battery not shown)

The rear sets help the rider to achieve a prone position

Pressed-steel spine frame – the engine is suspended beneath on rods

Distributor mounted behind the barrels

Werner Haas, twice world-title winner on Rennmaxes.

Perspex windscreen

Chin pad

Hand-formed alloy bodywork is shaped to suit the rider

The engine breather exits at the rear of the bike

Phenomenal performance meant that the opposition often enjoyed this handsome rear view of the Rennmax.

SPECIFICATIONS
NSU Rennmax
- **ENGINE** Double overhead-camshaft twin cylinder
- **BORE AND STROKE** 54 x 54mm (2⅛ x 2⅛in)
- **CAPACITY** 248cc
- **POWER OUTPUT** 36bhp @ 11,000rpm
- **CARBURATION** Two 25mm Fisher-Amals with remote float chamber
- **IGNITION** Battery and coil
- **TRANSMISSION** Four-speed (a six-speed was introduced in 1954), chain drive
- **CLUTCH** Dry multiplate
- **FRAME** Pressed-steel beam frame
- **SUSPENSION** Leading-link forks, rear swingarm
- **BRAKES** Drum brakes
- **WEIGHT** 117kg (258lb)
- **TOP SPEED** 210km/h (130mph)
- **YEAR OF CONSTRUCTION** 1953

Shock absorbers are mounted inside the pressed steel fork leg.

Leading-link forks

Alloy rims

The twin overhead cams are shaft driven

Air scoop keeps drum brakes cool

Components have holes drilled to reduce their weight

Other Classics

1938 Zündapp K800

Based in Nuremberg, Zündapp made a wide range of machines during sixty years of motorcycle manufacturing. The K800 was the largest bike that they built. The horizontally opposed four-cylinder engine was based on the more usual flat twin. Production of the flat four continued from 1933 to 1938. After the Second World War, Zündapp produced both flat twins and two-stroke designs. Twins were dropped in 1957 and production concentrated on two-stroke models. Zündapp won the 80cc World Championship in 1984 as well as many trials awards.

Hinged rear mudguard allows the wheel to be removed easily

Pressed-steel frame

Four-speed chain drive gearbox with gate change

Suspension damper knob

Pressed-steel girder forks

A heat shield protects the rider's legs

The carburettor, mounted above the crankcase, feeds the cylinders via a convoluted inlet track

Speedometer is mounted in the headlight

Victoria

Founded in 1886 as a bicycle factory, Victoria first built motorcycles in 1899. Many engine configurations and sizes were used. Victoria's Bergmeister was a shaft-driven V-twin foreshadowing the Moto Guzzi layout to follow 15 years later. In 1958 Victoria joined with DKW and Express in the Zweirad Union.

Carburettor cowl

Valanced front mudguard

Neutral selection lever

Plunger rear suspension

1955 Horex Imperator
- **ENGINE** Overhead-camshaft four-stroke twin
- **CAPACITY** 398cc
- **POWER OUTPUT** 24bhp @ 5,650rpm
- **TRANSMISSION** Four-speed gearbox, chain drive
- **FRAME** Tubular steel cradle
- **SUSPENSION** Schnell leading-link forks, rear swingarm
- **WEIGHT** 175kg (386lb)
- **TOP SPEED** 136km/h (84mph)

1955 Horex Imperator

The Horex Imperator was one of the most advanced machines of its time. Introduced in 1954, the 400cc twin-cylinder bike had many innovative features. Horex started producing bikes in 1928 but became a victim of the recession in the German motorcycle market in the late 1950s. The factory closed in 1958.

Elegant rear light and mudguard detail

Leading-link Schnell forks

Chrome covers hide the axle and suspension arms

Unit construction overhead-camshaft motor

Heel and toe gear lever

Enclosed chain

Gearbox cooling duct

Racing Kreidler, below without its fairing

Carburettor

Twelve-speed gearbox

1963 Kreidler Renn Florett

Kreidler concentrated on 50cc machines, steadily developing and improving design and performance. They expected to do well in the 50cc World Championship introduced in 1962, however Japanese makers produced more sophisticated and powerful machinery. Japan's withdrawal from racing in 1968, and changes in race rules in 1969, gave Kreidler their chance. In 1971 they won the first of six 50cc titles.

1963 Kreidler Renn Florett
- **ENGINE** Single-cylinder two stroke
- **CAPACITY** 49.9cc
- **POWER OUTPUT** 14bhp @ 15,000rpm
- **TRANSMISSION** Twelve-speed (four gears and three overdrives), chain drive
- **FRAME** Tubular steel cradle
- **SUSPENSION** Telescopic forks, rear swingarm
- **WEIGHT** 91kg (200lb) (estimated)
- **TOP SPEED** 170km/h (106mph)

Hans-Georg Anscheidt raced successfully for Kreidler in 1962 and 1963.

The lean tank is typical of 50cc racers

Leading-axle telescopic forks

KREIDLER

Florett

1

Wheel-balancing wire is wrapped around the spokes

Slim tyres minimize rolling resistance

Simple expansion chamber

Two-piece alloy fairing

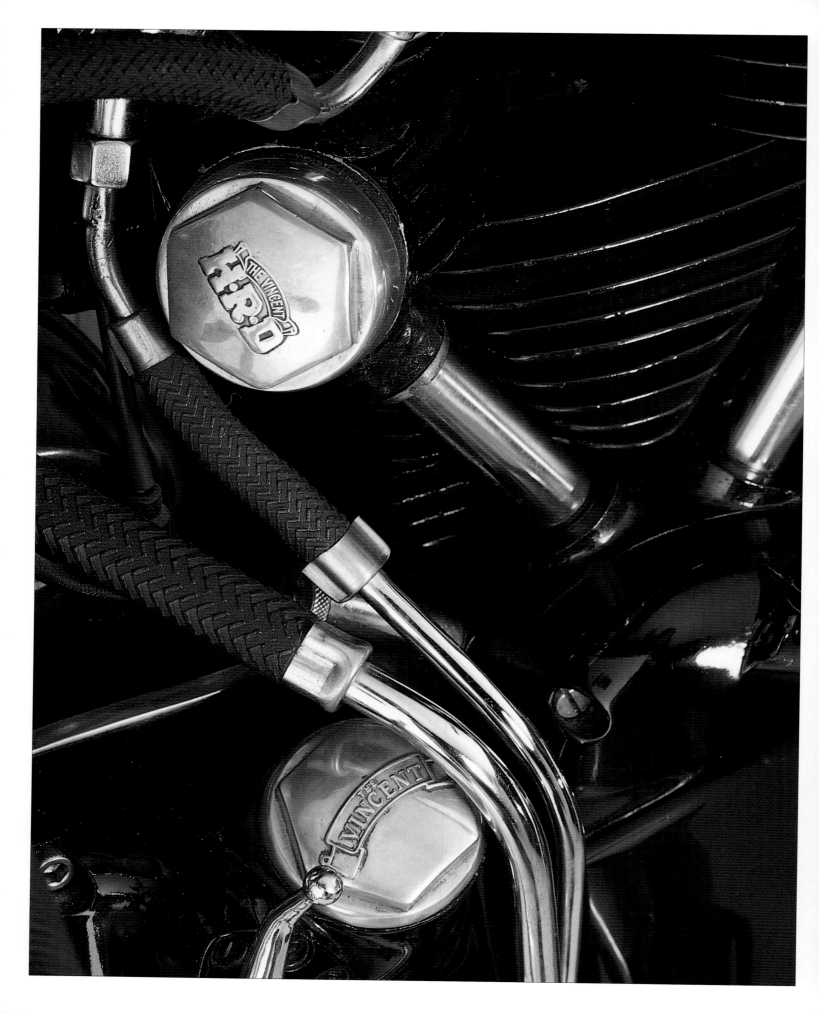

Great Britain

The British motorcycle industry, once a melting pot of innovation and manufacturing excellence, collapsed in the late seventies.

The first motorcycles built in Britain appeared in 1896 and included the unconventional Holden and the Excelsior, powered by a De Dion engine (p.10). Wrangling over patents and copyrights affected the development of new ideas and machines but the growth of the industry followed the same pattern as elsewhere in the world. Bicycle makers began fitting engines into modified pedal cycles; these firms included Triumph (pp.74-7), Sunbeam (p.86), Matchless (pp.64-5), and Enfield (p.87). Other firms with relevant expertise followed them: gun makers BSA (pp.68-9), chain-maker James Lansdowne Norton (p.70), and screw manufacturer A.J. Stevens (pp.64-5). These firms all became established and went on to enjoy a long history while hundreds more came and went. The majority of these pioneering companies were based around Coventry and Birmingham. This location, known as "the workshop of the world", continued to be the centre of the British motorcycle industry until its collapse, in the seventies.

Graham Walker's race helmet

Designing for Race and Road
The opening of the world's first purpose-built race track at Brooklands in 1907, and the annual Isle of Man TT races, challenged the developing industry to produce new and effective designs. When the First World War broke out, the shape and form of the motorcycle was established and ready for refinement. The industry too was well-established and, during the war, thousands of machines were supplied to the Armed Forces. In the inter-war years some remarkable machines were built: Edward Turner's Ariel Square Four (p.85), the 1937 Triumph Speed Twin (p.74), and the overhead-camshaft Norton single designed by Walter Moore in 1927. Experimental designs came from innovative firms like New Imperial and Excelsior, in addition to fast, luxurious, large-capacity motorcycles produced by George Brough (pp.66-7) and Philip Vincent (pp.82-3).

After the Second World War, Britain's motorcycle industry enjoyed a boom time. Their machines sold well at home and in America.

The Decline of the Empire
Lack of investment in design development and an unwillingness to change to genuine mass production put British makers at a disadvantage. Britain gradually lost its lead on the race tracks of the world but manufacturers did little to reverse the situation; complacency had set in. By the mid-fifties, the bulk of the British industry was controlled by two companies. Associated Motor Cycles incorporated AJS, Matchless, Norton, and the lesser-known James and Francis-Barnett marques. The conglomerate, BSA, absorbed Ariel, Triumph, and BSA. Four-stroke singles and vertical twins emerged as typical British bikes but many machines were based on pre-war designs with increased engine capacity to provide better performance. These machines handled well but were notoriously unreliable and vibrated severely at high speeds. Threatened by the arrival of superior small-capacity Japanese bikes, British makers retreated into the more profitable "big bike" market.

The BSA logo

Vincent HRD

The Matchless insignia

Sole Survivors
The end came swiftly. In the late sixties British manufacturers were building 70,000 machines a year. A decade later the only significant representative of the British motorcycle industry was the Triumph Bonneville, built by the workers' co-operative that took over the Triumph factory. Relaunched in 1992, Triumph now produces machines from a new factory quite unrelated to the old firm, and Norton's name has since reappeared affixed to a range of Wankel-engined machines.

1923 Temple-Anzani record breaker

AJS & Matchless

Harry Collier (foreground), and his brother Charlie Collier, won many races for Matchless, the family firm.

FOUNDED IN 1899, Matchless were amongst the first British motorcycle manufacturers. In 1931 they took over AJS and formed Associated Motor Cycles. Norton (pp.70-73) joined the group after the war. AMC collapsed in 1966. In the restructuring that followed, Norton's name took precedence; large-scale production of AJS and Matchless machines ceased.

Norton (pp.70-73)

SPECIFICATIONS

1933 Matchless Silver Hawk
- ENGINE Overhead-camshaft V-four
- CAPACITY 592cc
- POWER OUTPUT 26bhp
- TRANSMISSION Four-speed hand-change gearbox, chain drive
- FRAME Tubular cradle
- SUSPENSION Girder forks, cantilever rear
- WEIGHT 380lb (172kg)
- TOP SPEED 80mph (129km/h)

1933 Matchless Silver Hawk

The Silver Hawk was designed as a luxury touring machine to rival Ariel's Square Four (p.85). About five hundred bikes were built before production was stopped in 1935 – the market was too small to be profitable.

(p.85)

Cantilever rear suspension

Gearchange lever

Silver M tank badge

Coupled brakes

Fishtail exhaust

Skew-gear driven dynamo

Shaft-driven overhead camshaft

Oil tank for dry sump engine

SPECIFICATIONS

1939 AJS Supercharged V-four
- ENGINE Single overhead-camshaft supercharged 50° V-four
- CAPACITY 495cc
- POWER OUTPUT 80bhp (estimated)
- TRANSMISSION Four-speed gearbox, chain drive
- FRAME Tubular cradle duplex
- SUSPENSION Girder forks, rear plunger with friction damper
- WEIGHT 405lb (184kg)
- TOP SPEED 135mph (217km/h)

1939 AJS Supercharged V-four

The V-four AJS was built to take on the supercharged continental bikes that dominated the Grand Prix just before the war. It was the first machine ever to lap a Grand Prix course at over 100mph (160km/h).

Friction damped plunger suspension

Chest pad

Radiator

Oil tank

Supercharger

1941 Matchless G3L

These bikes were typical British single-cylinder machines. Over eighty thousand Matchless singles were built for the British forces during the Second World War, and civilian versions of these models remained popular for many years afterwards. The G3L was one of the first British motorcycles to feature hydraulically damped telescopic forks.

Matchless motorcycles were first built in Woolwich, London.

Pannier racks

Sprung saddle

Identification number

Black-out lighting

Speedometer driven from back wheel

Military bikes were painted all over

Bikes for desert action were buff-coloured

Army motorcycles were required to be rugged and reliable in all conditions.

Oil damped telescopic forks

SPECIFICATIONS
1941 Matchless G3L
- **ENGINE** Overhead-valve vertical single
- **CAPACITY** 347cc
- **POWER OUTPUT** 16.6bhp
- **TRANSMISSION** Four-speed gearbox, chain drive
- **FRAME** Cradle
- **SUSPENSION** Telescopic forks
- **WEIGHT** 392lb (134kg)
- **TOP SPEED** 70mph (113km/h) (estimated)

Bob Foster prepares his AJS blown four at the Isle of Man TT races.

SPECIFICATIONS
1948 AJS 7R
- **ENGINE** Overhead-camshaft single-cylinder four-stroke
- **CAPACITY** 349cc
- **POWER OUTPUT** 31bhp @ 7,000rpm
- **TRANSMISSION** Four-speed gearbox, chain drive
- **FRAME** Duplex cradle
- **SUSPENSION** Telescopic forks , rear swingarm
- **WEIGHT** 298lb (135kg)
- **TOP SPEED** 110mph (177km/h)

1948 AJS 7R

Based on the pre-war Model 7 design, the 7R was popular with private racers. It was straightforward in its construction, and simple to maintain. The first 7Rs were built in 1948 and remained in production until 1962.

Megaphone exhausts produced greater power, but they also increased the noise made by the machine.

Burman four-speed gearbox

Mag alloy components are painted gold

Brough Superior

W.E. BROUGH BEGAN BUILDING motorcycles in Nottingham in 1908, and his son George followed him into the business. After a family disagreement, George Brough set up Brough Superior in 1921. Brough's expensive, powerful machines were advertised as the "Rolls Royce of motorcycles". In addition to the superb V-twins, Brough built prototypes and a few exclusive production models, including the "Golden Dream" of 1938, powered by a four-cylinder twin-crank engine. Brough stopped building motorcycles in 1940 and switched to production of aircraft components as part of the war effort. They never built motorcycles again.

T. E. Lawrence was George Brough's most famous client. He owned a succession of SS100s all of which he named "George" after his friend George Bernard Shaw. Lawrence died in 1935 after an accident while riding his Brough.

1930 Brough Superior SS100 Alpine Grand Sport
The most sophisticated SS100 model ever built, the Alpine Sport featured rear suspension and twin magnetos. The machine was named after the Alpine Rally in which George Brough won a gold medal on the prototype machine. Based on the conventional SS100, the Alpine Grand Sport was better equipped and featured many uprated components.

Panniers

Rear suspension is by cantilever fork with the springs under the seat

Friction damper

Back brake adjuster

Three-speed Sturmey-Archer gearbox

A chrome cover hides two Lucas combined magneto/dynamos

A close-up look at the left-hand side of the engine shows the exposed valve springs and twin float bowls (the single carburettor has two float bowls). SS100 models used overhead valves and guaranteed a 100mph (160km/h) top speed. Side-valve SS80s were 20mph (32km/h) slower.

Exposed valve springs

Twin float bowls

Oil-tank filler cap

Fly screen

The inverted handlebar levers pivot at the end of the bars

The stainless-steel saddle tank holds 4 gallons (18 litres)

Brough's Castle forks are modelled on a Harley-Davidson design

Hand-change gear lever and linkage to gearbox

Horn

The wheels are the same size front and rear

This particular model has a JAP engine, though some SS80s and SS100s used engines made by Matchless

Pilgrim oil pump

SPECIFICATIONS

SS100 Alpine Grand Sports

- **ENGINE** Overhead-valve 50° V-twin JAP engine
- **BORE AND STROKE** 3¹⁄₁₀ x 3⅜in (80 x 99mm)
- **CAPACITY** 998cc
- **POWER OUTPUT** 45hp (estimated)
- **CARBURATION** Brough double float chambers
- **IGNITION** Magneto
- **TRANSMISSION** Four-speed Sturmey-Archer hand-change gearbox, chain drive
- **CLUTCH** Six-spring clutch
- **FRAME** Tubular cradle
- **SUSPENSION** Castle leading-link forks, Bentley & Draper cantilever rear forks
- **BRAKES** Drum brakes, front and rear
- **WEIGHT** 400lb (181kg)
- **TOP SPEED** 100mph (161km/h)
- **YEAR OF CONSTRUCTION** 1930

BSA

T HE BIRMINGHAM SMALL ARMS COMPANY built their first motorcycles in 1906, and became Britain's biggest manufacturer. BSA bikes were generally solid and reliable rather than innovative, and the firm rarely sanctioned racing. After the Second World War, BSA were the biggest motorcycle company in the world, but during the 1960s Japanese machines eroded BSA's markets. By 1970, BSA were in trouble. The firm was absorbed into the Norton-Villiers-Triumph group (pp.70-77), and the BSA name was finally abandoned in 1973.

Reliable, and excellent for sidecar use, one of BSA's V-twins features in a 1920s advertisement.

Flat-sided tank design

Tool bag

Magneto ignition

Cast aluminium chain case

Dummy belt rim brakes

1920 BSA Model E
The Model E was introduced at the end of 1919, the first of a series of BSA V-twins that were produced between the wars. Although the engine design was unremarkable, the machines were cheap, reliable, and popular, especially for use with sidecars.

SPECIFICATIONS
1921 BSA Model E
- ENGINE Side-valve V-twin
- CAPACITY 770cc
- POWER OUTPUT 6hp
- TRANSMISSION Three-speed gearbox, chain drive
- FRAME Tubular diamond pattern
- SUSPENSION Girder forks
- WEIGHT 336lb (152.5kg)
- TOP SPEED 55mph (88.5km/h) (estimated)

SPECIFICATIONS
1930 BSA Sloper
- ENGINE Overhead-valve single-cylinder
- CAPACITY 493cc
- POWER OUTPUT 20bhp (estimated)
- TRANSMISSION Three-speed handchange gearbox, chain drive
- FRAME Bolt-up cradle with forged I-section top member
- SUSPENSION Girder forks
- WEIGHT 337lb (153kg)
- TOP SPEED 70-75mph (113-20km/h)

1930 BSA Sloper
The introduction of the Sloper (which was given this name because of its inclined cylinder) marked a change of direction for BSA's designs. This eye-catching and unusually quiet sporting machine set new standards in motorcycle construction and style. The public loved the Sloper, and the bike sold in large numbers.

Hand change gears

Chrome saddle-tank

Twin-port cylinder head

Integral oil tank

Three factory riders won gold medals in the International Six Days Trial on BSA Star Twins in 1932.

1952 BSA A7 500cc Star Twin

BSA's contender for the twin-cylinder market was launched in 1946. In 1950, a 650 version appeared. Both remained in production until the new, unit-construction models were developed in 1962.

This is one of the three historic Maudes Trophy bikes, subjected to an observed 4, 958-mile (7,979km) test in 1952.

Plunger rear suspension

SPECIFICATIONS

1952 BSA Star Twin
- **ENGINE** Overhead-valve vertical twin
- **CAPACITY** 498cc
- **POWER OUTPUT** 27.4bhp
- **TRANSMISSION** Four-speed gearbox, chain drive
- **FRAME** Cradle
- **SUSPENSION** Telescopic forks, plunger unit rear
- **WEIGHT** 382lb (173kg)
- **TOP SPEED** 85mph (137km/h)

Pre-unit design has engine and gearbox separate

Amal GP carburettor

BSA Gold Star badge

1960 BSA Gold Star DBD34

The Gold Star is the most famous of all the BSA machines. It became a favourite with aspiring competition riders in the 1950s, and many still regard it as the ultimate British single.

All-alloy engine

Swept-back exhaust pipe

SPECIFICATIONS

1960 BSA Gold Star DBD34
- **ENGINE** Overhead-valve single-cylinder
- **CAPACITY** 499cc
- **POWER OUTPUT** 40bhp @ 7,000rpm
- **TRANSMISSION** Four-speed gearbox, chain drive
- **FRAME** Tubular cradle
- **SUSPENSION** Telescopic forks, rear swingarm
- **WEIGHT** 308lb (140kg)
- **TOP SPEED** 110mph (177kmh)

SPECIFICATIONS

1966 BSA A65 Lightning Clubman
- **ENGINE** Overhead-valve parallel twin
- **CAPACITY** 654cc
- **POWER OUTPUT** 53bhp @ 7,000rpm
- **TRANSMISSION** Four-speed gearbox, chain drive
- **FRAME** Tubular cradle
- **SUSPENSION** Telescopic forks, rear swingarm
- **WEIGHT** 421lb (191kg)
- **TOP SPEED** 115mph (185km/h)

1966 BSA A65 Lightning Clubman

This is a special sporting version of BSA's new twin-cylinder machines that appeared in 1962. Although a fine machine, it never achieved the same acclaim as equivalent Triumph or Norton models.

Steering damper

Twin carburettors

Chrome headlight

Rear sprocket is mounted on the brake drum

Both cylinders exit into one silencer

Unit engine design

Norton

NORTON'S IMPRESSIVE REPUTATION was founded on their considerable success on the race track. Their earliest motorcycles were fitted with proprietary engines; a Norton with a V-twin Peugeot engine won the twin-cylinder class at the first TT in 1907. The first engine to carry Norton's own name, a single-cylinder design, was produced in 1908. The company went on to develop a wide variety of singles – from racers and touring bikes to simple workhorse machines. Then, in 1948, Norton built their first parallel twin.

James Lansdowne Norton started his motorcycle business in 1901. He died in 1925, aged 56.

The Whittle drive belt is made of leather pieces riveted together

1912 Norton BS "Old Miracle"

In 1911, Norton's 490cc side-valve engine was used in this famous machine. "Old Miracle" could lap the Brooklands track at 70mph (113km/h), and set 112 national speed records between 1912 and 1920. It was the prototype for Norton's Brooklands Special.

Bicycle-type stirrup brakes

Knee pads

The main stand pivots at the end of the rigid frame.

490cc side-valve Norton engine

Chain-driven magneto

SPECIFICATIONS

1912 Norton BS "Old Miracle"
- •ENGINE Side-valve single cylinder
- •CAPACITY 490cc
- •POWER OUTPUT 3½hp
- •TRANSMISSION Single speed, belt drive
- •FRAME Diamond pattern
- •SUSPENSION Girder forks
- •WEIGHT 250lb (113kg) (estimated)
- •TOP SPEED 70mph (113km/h)

1927 Norton Model 18

Norton's first overhead-valve singles were produced in 1922, and in 1924 the design won the TT. The Model 18 made its appearance at the same time. It remained in the Norton catalogue until 1954, but other ohv singles were still in production in the 1960s.

Exposed rocker arms and valve springs

Flat-sided tank

Oil tank

SPECIFICATIONS

1927 Norton Model 18
- •ENGINE Overhead-valve single
- •CAPACITY 490cc
- •POWER OUTPUT 18bhp (estimated)
- •TRANSMISSION Sturmey-Archer three-speed gearbox, chain drive
- •FRAME Tubular cradle with engine as stressed member
- •SUSPENSION Single-spring girder forks
- •WEIGHT 336lb (152kg)
- •TOP SPEED 80mph (129km/h) (quoted in a contemporary road test)

Twin-chambered fishtail silencer

1962 Norton Manx 30M

Norton's overhead-camshaft singles were first made in 1927 and were refined over the next thirty years. Production stopped in the early 1960s. "Featherbed"-framed models, such as the one shown below, enjoyed superior handling, and competed well against more powerful bikes.

Petrol tank retraining strap

A flyscreen protects the rider

Rev counter

Shortened race-style mudguards

Flattened megaphone exhaust allows steeper cornering angles

Central oil tank

The deeply-finned cylinder barrel increases the cooling effect

A double-loop tubular frame, produces the famous "Featherbed" ride

Twin leading-shoe ventilated drum brake with air scoops

1962 Norton 650SS Dominator

Following the success of the Triumph Speed Twin (p.74), Norton built their own 500cc parallel twin in 1948. Thirty years later, the final Norton twins were based on this design, though the capacity was increased to 828cc. The 650SS was built from 1962 until 1970.

Norton Roadholder forks

Angled carburettors

Chrome grab-rail

Chrome mudguard

Primary drive chaincase

Norton Commando

AFTER THE SECOND WORLD WAR, Norton had a turbulent time. Associated Motor Cycles, including AJS and Matchless (pp. 64-5), bought Norton in 1953. The group was taken over in 1966 by Manganese Bronze Holdings, who chose to promote the Norton name in preference to AJS or Matchless. BSA and Triumph then joined Norton in the Norton-Villiers-Triumph Group. Norton's twin design had become dated, but the projected replacement never reached production. NVT eventually went to the wall in 1977, but the Norton name was saved and small-scale manufacture of Wankel-engined motorcycles began in the early 1980s.

1969 Norton Fastback Commando
The Commando's chassis incorporated "Isolastic" engine mountings, which reduced the vibration from the 750cc engine to acceptable levels without compromising Norton's reputation for excellent handling. Although popular, the Commando was not as refined or reliable as its Japanese competitors: even the introduction of an 850cc version and an electric starter in the 1970s could not save the marque. The last Commandos were built in 1977.

Primary chaincase

The Commando's performance was enhanced by its slim profile and light weight.

"Fastback" tail-piece

The fuel tank is made of glass fibre

Air filter

750 COMMANDO

Pre-unit four-speed gearbox

DID YOU KNOW?

The Norton Commando was voted "Machine of the Year" for five years in succession from 1968 to 1972, in a poll conducted in Britain by *Motor Cycle News* magazine.

The famous Norton logo has remained unchanged, evoking the longevity of the marque

To overcome the Commando engine's power deficit, Norton's Formula 750 racers had to be lighter and more aerodynamic, and handle better, than their competitors. This was achieved by clever chassis design. The monocoque frame shown here was designed, developed, and ridden by Peter Williams. A fuel pump is operated by movement of the rear swingarm. The bike was very successful despite a 25bhp disadvantage. This 1973 version uses a steel monocoque in which the fuel is housed in pannier fuel tanks.

A header tank feeds the carburettors

The petrol tank is contained within the monocoque chassis

Oil cooler

Forward-mounted oil tank

Cast alloy wheels

Glass-fibre seat

JOHN PLAYER NORTON

10

Peel-style fairing

Peter Williams won the 1973 Formula 750 TT on a Norton Commando works' racer.

Pushrod tunnels are cast into the iron barrel

Engine, gearbox, and swingarm are mounted on "Isolastic" bushes

Front mounted number plates were discontinued in the U.K. during the 1970s

Twin leading-shoe drum brake

SPECIFICATIONS

Norton Fastback Commando

- **ENGINE** Overhead-valve parallel twin
- **BORE AND STROKE** 2¾ x 3½in (73 x 89mm)
- **CAPACITY** 745cc
- **POWER OUTPUT** 56bhp @ 6500rpm
- **CARBURATION** Twin Amal concentric carburettors
- **IGNITION** Battery and coil
- **TRANSMISSION** Four-speed gearbox, chain drive
- **CLUTCH** Six-plate wet clutch
- **FRAME** Tubular cradle with Isolastic mounted engine and rear swingarm
- **SUSPENSION** Telescopic forks, rear swingarm
- **BRAKES** Twin leading-shoe front drum brakes, single leading-shoe rear drum brakes
- **WEIGHT** 398lb (180kg)
- **TOP SPEED** 115mph (185km/h)
- **YEAR OF CONSTRUCTION** 1969

Triumph

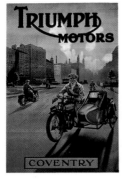

A 1920's poster shows a Triumph and sidecar.

TRIUMPH, ONE OF THE MOST FAMOUS bike builders, was founded in Britain by two Germans, Siegfried Bettman and Mauritz Schulte, who set up the company in 1897 to build bicycles. They produced their first motorbike in 1902, and this was followed by a variety of machines, ranging from a 225cc two-stroke to 500cc four-valve singles. In 1936 Triumph came under the same ownership as the Ariel company (p.85) and a new designer, Edward Turner from Ariel, was appointed. Turner updated many of the existing designs, and was responsible for their most significant creation, the legendary Speed Twin that became the basis for Triumph's big bikes until the 1980s.

1923 Triumph Model R Fast Roadster
Harry (later Sir Harry) Ricardo designed the cylinder head and barrel that were added to Triumph's popular Model H to form the Model R. The new head was of an innovative four-valve design perfected by Honda forty years later.

1939 Triumph Speed Twin
The Speed Twin appeared in 1937. It was not the first parallel twin, but no earlier machine had the impact of the new Triumph. Designed by Edward Turner, the Speed Twin and its derivatives formed the basis of the Triumph range for the next forty years.

Inverted handlebar levers

Hand gearchange

"Druid" style girder forks

The rear brake acts on a dummy pulley

Four-valve engine

Chain-driven magneto

Bicycle-type stirrup brakes

Tank-top instrument and control panel

Sprung saddle

Casing for oil pump and timing gears

Chain adjustment bolts

SPECIFICATIONS
1923 Model R Fast Roadster
- **ENGINE** Overhead four-valve single
- **CAPACITY** 499cc
- **POWER OUTPUT** 20bhp
- **TRANSMISSION** Three-speed handchange gearbox, chain drive
- **FRAME** Tubular diamond pattern
- **SUSPENSION** Girder forks, no rear suspension
- **WEIGHT** 240lb (109kg)
- **TOP SPEED** 70-75mph (113-21km/h)

1959 Triumph Bonneville

The most famous Triumph of them all, this high-performance production model was named after the Salt Flats where Johnny Allen broke the World Land Speed Record in 1955 (pp.78-9).

Distinctive Triumph headlight nacelle

Speedometer

An overhead view shows the controls and the tank-top luggage rack.

Four-speed gearbox

Twin carburettors with separate float bowl

Single down-tube frame

SPECIFICATIONS

1959 Triumph Bonneville
- •ENGINE Overhead-valve vertical twin
- •CAPACITY 649cc
- •POWER OUTPUT 46bhp @ 6,500rpm
- •TRANSMISSION Four-speed gearbox, chain drive
- •FRAME Tubular cradle
- •SUSPENSION Telescopic forks, rear swingarm
- •WEIGHT 404lb (183kg)
- •TOP SPEED 110mph (177km/h)

1966 Triumph Bonneville TT Special

The American market was important to Triumph, and other British firms, in the 1950s and 1960s. As off-road riding was very popular in America, this model, designed for export, came without lights or silencers. In later years the market for off-road bikes came to be dominated by lightweight Japanese machines.

Engine "kill" button

This tank design was created for the export market

Air filters

Rubber gaiters to protect fork legs

Off-road tyres

Unit engine and gearbox construction

Painted wheel rim centre

SPECIFICATIONS

1939 Triumph Speed Twin
- •ENGINE Vertical overhead-valve twin
- •CAPACITY 498cc
- •POWER OUTPUT 26bhp @ 6,000rpm
- •TRANSMISSION Four-speed gearbox, chain drive
- •FRAME Tubular cradle
- •SUSPENSION Girder forks, no rear suspension
- •WEIGHT 378lb (171.5 kg)
- •TOP SPEED 94mph (151km/h)

SPECIFICATIONS

1966 Bonneville TT Special
- •ENGINE Vertical overhead-valve twin
- •CAPACITY 649cc
- •POWER OUTPUT 54bhp @ 6,500rpm
- •TRANSMISSION Four-speed unit gearbox, chain drive
- •FRAME Duplex cradle
- •SUSPENSION Telescopic forks, rear swingarm
- •WEIGHT 350lb (158.8 kg)
- •TOP SPEED 130mph (209km/h)

Marlon Brando rode a Triumph Thunderbird, an enlarged version of the renowned Speed Twin, for his leading role in the 1954 film *The Wild One.*

Triumph Trident

W HEN T RIUMPH WAS bought by BSA (pp.68-9) in 1951, the two companies maintained their separate identities. During the next twenty years, Triumph prospered and remained the biggest-selling import in the lucrative American market. The British industry shrank in the 1970s, and BSA-Triumph became part of the Norton-Villiers-Triumph Group. All mass-produced British motorcycles were handled by the group. During the takeover, Triumph employees occupied the factory as a workers' co-operative and restarted production of the long-lived Bonneville model. N.V.T. collapsed, but the manufacture of Bonnevilles continued for some years afterwards. The Triumph co-operative folded in August 1983; the name changed hands again. Production then resumed in 1990, at a new factory in Leicestershire, using designs inspired by the Japanese.

Steve McQueen's bike collection included several Triumphs.

1969 Triumph T150 Trident

The Triumph Trident beat the four-cylinder 750 Honda on to the superbike market by just a few months, but could not match the Honda's refined features. Later versions of the model were made with electric starters, disc brakes, and five-speed gearboxes, but still featured the original Trident's excellent handling and gutsy power delivery. However, this new-found sophistication was not enough to save the model from extinction as a result of Japanese competition; production of Tridents stopped in 1975.

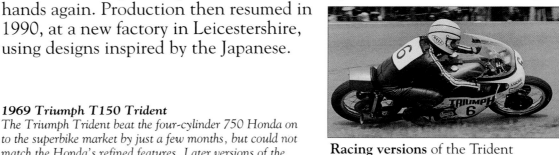

Racing versions of the Trident dominated the 750 class. In 1972, Ray Pickrell won the Formula 750 TT; his average speed over the five laps was 104mph (168km/h).

Front brake air scoop

Grab rail

Saddle-release knob

Oil cooler with side reflectors attached

These unusual exhausts were nicknamed "ray gun" silencers

The horn is on the down tube

The engine is based on the 500cc Twin, but with an added cylinder

The gear change is on the right

SPECIFICATIONS

1973 Triumph X75 Hurricane
- **ENGINE** Transverse overhead-valve triple
- **CAPACITY** 740cc
- **POWER OUTPUT** 58bhp @ 7,250rpm
- **TRANSMISSION** Four-speed gearbox, chain drive
- **FRAME** Duplex cradle
- **SUSPENSION** Telescopic forks, rear swingarm
- **WEIGHT** 444lb (201kg)
- **TOP SPEED** 105-10mph (169-77km/h)

1972 Triumph Hurricane
BSA-Triumph commissioned American designer Craig Vetter to style a special limited production version of their three-cylinder motorcycle for the American market. The machine's running gear was standard, apart from lower gearing. Some cosmetic modifications were made; these included the one-piece seat and tank, distinctive three-pipe exhaust system, and extended forks. Japanese manufacturers took up the idea of producing "Factory custom" machines a few years later.

The spectacular Hurricane was built in limited numbers and has now become a collector's bike.

Oil tank

Small-capacity fuel tank

Feed pipes for rockers

The forks have been extended by 1in (2.5cm)

Triple "swept-up" silencers

The conical-hub front brake was notoriously poor

Ignition lock

Zener diode charging regulator

Twin leading-shoe ventilated front drum

SPECIFICATIONS

1969 Triumph Trident T150
- **ENGINE** Transverse overhead-valve triple
- **CAPACITY** 740cc
- **POWER OUTPUT** 58bhp @ 7,250rpm
- **TRANSMISSION** Four-speed gearbox, chain drive
- **FRAME** Tubular cradle
- **SUSPENSION** Telescopic forks, rear swingarm
- **WEIGHT** 482lb (219kg)
- **TOP SPEED** 122mph (196km/h)

go modern go TRIUMPH

Triumph's 1966 sales brochure emphasizes advanced design and technology. In reality, the bikes were out-dated when launched, and soon lost the market lead.

THE NEW TRIDENT

Launched in 1990, the new Trident features a twelve-valve, three-cylinder, water-cooled engine with double overhead camshafts. The familiar old Triumph logo has been subtly amended: on the tank of the new model, the wide, flamboyant upward sweep of the tail of the stylized letter "R" now stops just short of the final "H" of Triumph.

Single shock rear suspension

Engine and exhausts are finished in black

Large-capacity radiator

Speed Records

LAND SPEED RECORDS ATTRACTED worldwide publicity and had great prestige before jet power made everyone complacent about speed. In America, the 100mph (161km/h) barrier was officially broken by Lee Humiston aboard an Excelsior (p.41) as early as 1913; in Britain it was not until 1921 that Douglas Davidson first achieved a speed record of 100.76mph (162.1km/h) aboard a Harley-Davidson at Brooklands. Disagreements between the governing bodies of motorcycle sport mean that American and European official records sometimes vary. As speeds increased, the locations for the record attempts changed. Record-breakers soon moved from closed roads and banked race tracks, to the open space of the Bonneville Salt Flats in Utah, western USA.

Triumph derived considerable publicity from Johnny Allen's 1956 world speed record.

The Bonneville Salt Flats are still a Mecca for record-breaking motorcyclists. Official meetings are held twice each year.

Johnny Allen on his way to the record in 1956. Speeds are calculated from an average of two runs.

--- DID YOU KNOW? ---
Donald A. Vesco of America and the 21ft (6.4m) "Lightning Bolt" streamliner, powered by two 1016cc Kawasaki engines, set the AMA and FIM absolute world speed records with an overall average of 318.598mph (512.733km/h) on Bonneville Salt Flats, Utah, on 28 August 1978.

1956 Triumph Record Breaker
The machines used to attack the speed record now bear no resemblance to a conventional motorcycle. An American team using this cigar-shaped projectile achieved a speed of 214.4mph (345km/h) at Bonneville in 1956. This record was not ratified by the FIM (Federation of International Motorcyclists), despite the fact that the timekeeper and his equipment had been approved before the record attempt. Triumph had the last laugh when the company named its most famous model (pp.74-5) after the Salt Flats.

SPECIFICATIONS

1956 Triumph Record-Breaker
- **ENGINE** Modified Triumph Thunderbird air-cooled overhead-valve twin
- **CAPACITY** 649cc
- **POWER OUTPUT** 65bhp (estimated)
- **TRANSMISSION** Four-speed, chain drive
- **FRAME** All-welded space frame
- **SUSPENSION** Telescopic forks, rubber-band controlled rear swingarm
- **WEIGHT** Not disclosed
- **TOP SPEED** 214.4mph (345km/h)

The aluminium body shell is fitted to a tubular space-frame chassis

Aerodynamic bodywork

This model had an extraordinarily long wheelbase – 9ft 2½in (2.8 metres).

THE FIRST SPEED KINGS

Early record breakers were magnificent-looking machines, with the emphasis on the engine. This Temple-Anzani was built in 1923, during the golden era of the record-breaker. In October of that year, on the banked Brooklands track, it set a short-lived record of 108.48mph (174.6kmh). Two years later it won more lasting fame when rider and bike-builder Claude Temple became the first man to cover 100 miles (160km), in one hour on a motorcycle.

Claude Temple wore this crash helmet when racing at Brooklands.

Claude Temple at the Brooklands circuit

Fuel tank breather pipe

Sprung saddle

Harley-Davidson forks

Rear drum-brake

Oil tank

The tank and forks are copper-plated

Loop frame

Straight-through exhausts

The rider sits in the cockpit, with his legs straight out in front of him.

The exhaust pipe exit is flush with the bodywork

The 650cc triumph engine is positioned behind the rider

Timekeeper's identification number

"Chequered flag" tail-pattern so the machine can be sighted when passing at speed

Retractable stand

Velocette

VELOCE, FOUNDED IN 1904, built their first two-stroke "Velocettes" in 1913. Although the company subsequently returned to four-stroke production, the name was retained. In the forties and fifties, investment in the innovative LE model nearly crippled the company as sales were poor. The marque survived until 1971.

SPECIFICATIONS

1921 Velocette D2
- ENGINE Two-stroke single
- CAPACITY 220cc
- POWER OUTPUT 8bhp
- TRANSMISSION Two-speed countershaft
- FRAME Tubular cradle
- SUSPENSION Girder forks, rigid rear
- WEIGHT 158lb (71.5kg)
- TOP SPEED 40mph (64km/h)

Bath-tap gear lever

Brampton girder forks

Bicycle-style stirrup brakes

Advance/retard mechanism

Decompressor

1921 Velocette D2
The D2, with its overhung-crankshaft engine with separate oiling, is a superb example of a Velocette two-stroke. A ladies' model, fitted with a U-shaped frame, was available.

SPECIFICATIONS

1947 Velocette KTT Mark 8
- ENGINE Overhead camshaft single-cylinder four stroke
- CAPACITY 348cc
- POWER OUTPUT 34bhp
- TRANSMISSION Four-speed gearbox, chain drive
- FRAME Tubular steel cradle
- SUSPENSION Webb girder forks, rear swingarm
- WEIGHT 320lb (145kg)
- TOP SPEED 115mph (185km/h)

1947 Velocette KTT Mark 8
The first 350cc overhead-camshaft Velocettes were built in 1925, and for the next 25 years they won races throughout the world. The KTT Mark 8 was a production replica of the works racers that dominated the 1938 TT. Production models changed little after the war, but the factory used double overhead-camshaft specials to win the World Championship in 1949 and 1950.

Freddie Frith won the 350cc World Championship on a Velocette KTT in 1949.

The oil feedlines supply the camshaft drive and cylinder head

Oleo-pneumatic shock absorbers used air for springing

Magnesium-alloy conical brake hubs

1967 Velocette Thruxton Venom

Named after the Hampshire circuit where long-distance production bike races were held in the fifties and sixties, the Thruxton Venom was the most powerful version of Velocette's overhead-valve, single-cylinder design. A tuned version of the basic Venom model, the Thruxton won the 1967 500cc Production TT.

Clip-on handlebars

Amal GP carburettor

Slotted shock absorber mounts allow adjustment of the suspension

Fishtail silencer

Brazed lug frame

Twin leading-shoe brake

1960 Velocette LE Mark 3

The remarkable and revolutionary LE was launched in 1949. Velocette believed that its technically advanced specification would appeal to buyers, but in fact sales were very poor. A more conventional-looking, air-cooled version was produced, but this also failed to attract a significant number of private buyers.

The British Police adopted the LE with enthusiasm; its silent running and straightforward maintenance requirements were ideal qualities for police transport.

The fuel tank is housed within the pressed steel chassis

Metal panniers

Footshift gear lever. Earlier models used a handchange

Leg shields

Vincent HRD

PHILIP VINCENT bought the rights to HRD's name, and established his new firm in 1928. Exceptional quality and superb engineering made Vincents expensive, but highly desirable. Early models used JAP engines but, in 1935, Vincent designed their own 500cc overhead-valve single. This 500cc design was doubled up to produce the first of the famous V-twins. The pre-war bikes were nicknamed "the plumber's nightmare" due to their confusion of external oil pipes. Post-war machines were of a tidier and stronger design. The Vincent V-twin was the fastest machine of its day. Despite its high price tag, production became uneconomic, and was stopped in 1955.

HRD was founded by TT race winner Howard R. Davies in 1924. Philip Vincent bought the name in 1928 to give credibility to his new company.

1949 Vincent Black Shadow, Series C
Vincent claimed that their Black Shadow was "the world's fastest and safest standard motorcycle"; this was not an idle boast. The Black Shadow was a tuned version of the Rapide model. Visual changes were the baked-on black finish of the engine and a Smiths speedometer, reading up to 150mph (240km/h). The Series C was produced from 1949 to 1954.

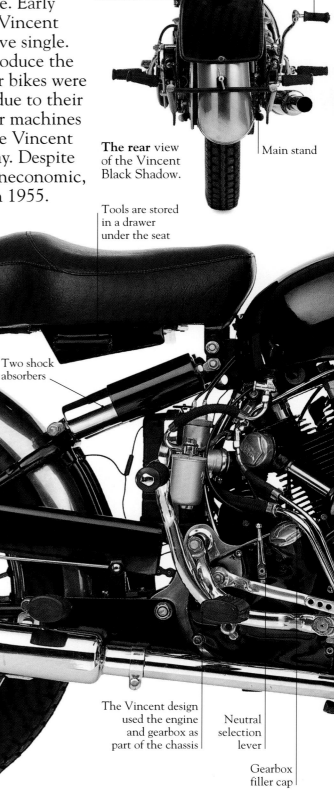

The handlebars are Vincent straights

Carburettor float bowl

Kick starter

Main stand

The rear view of the Vincent Black Shadow.

Tools are stored in a drawer under the seat

Two shock absorbers

The mudguards are made of stainless steel. Vincent hated chrome and used stainless steel on his bikes wherever possible

The Vincent design used the engine and gearbox as part of the chassis

Neutral selection lever

Gearbox filler cap

Rollie Free rode a Black Lightning at 157mph (252km/h) on Bonneville Salt Flats in 1948. He lay prone, dressed only in swimming trunks and gym shoes.

The front brakes are operated evenly by an ingenious cantilever beam system.

Decompressor

Brake operating beam

Siamese exhaust pipes

Axles with built-in tommy bars for wheel removal

Twin brakes

Smiths speedometer

Girdraulic forks

Rocker covers

Pushrod tube

SPECIFICATIONS

Vincent Black Shadow Series C

- ENGINE Overhead-camshaft, air-cooled, 50° V-twin four-stroke engine
- BORE AND STROKE 3¼ x 1½in (84 x 90mm)
- CAPACITY 998cc
- POWER OUTPUT 55bhp @ 5,700rpm
- CARBURATION 2 x 1⅛in (29mm) Amal standard carburettors
- IGNITION Lucas magneto
- TRANSMISSION Four-speed gearbox, chain drive
- CLUTCH Dry friction plate with servo shoes
- FRAME Box section spine with stressed engine
- SUSPENSION Girdraulic forks, cantilever rear
- BRAKES Twin 7in (17.8cm) drums, front and rear
- WEIGHT 458lb (208kg)
- TOP SPEED 122mph (196km/h)
- YEAR OF CONSTRUCTION 1949

This fine engine detail reveals the immaculate rocker covers, push-rod tube, neutral selection lever, and gearbox filler-cap.

Black engine cases display the Vincent HRD logo

A side stand is fitted to both sides. When used with the main stand, both wheels can be lifted clear of the ground for maintenance

Two drum brakes are fitted to each wheel

Other Classics

1932 Douglas K32

Famous for their high-quality, flat-twin engines, Douglas built many capacity variations on the basic flat-twin layout. In 1922, a Douglas was the first machine to exceed 100mph (160km/h) in Britain.

The painted panel of the fuel tank is framed with the Douglas tartan

SPECIFICATIONS
1932 Douglas K32
- **ENGINE** Overhead-valve horizontally-opposed twin
- **CAPACITY** 348cc
- **POWER OUTPUT** 12-15bhp (estimated)
- **TRANSMISSION** Three-speed hand-change gearbox, chain drive
- **FRAME** Duplex cradle
- **SUSPENSION** Girder forks, rigid rear
- **WEIGHT** 255lb (116kg)
- **TOP SPEED** 65mph (105km/h) (estimated)

Centrally sprung girder-forks

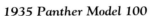

Single carburettor

The gearbox is mounted above the engine to keep the wheelbase short

SPECIFICATIONS
1935 Panther Model 100
- **ENGINE** Overhead-valve inclined single
- **CAPACITY** 598cc
- **POWER OUTPUT** 26bhp
- **TRANSMISSION** Four-speed Burman, chain drive
- **FRAME** Tubular with engine as stressed member
- **SUSPENSION** Girder forks, rigid rear
- **WEIGHT** 353lb (160kg)
- **TOP SPEED** 85mph (137km/h)

1935 Panther Model 100

As a company, Phelon and Moore did not undertake change lightly: their final machines, built in 1966, were directly related to their first "sloping singles" built at the turn of the century. The bikes were not very powerful, but they were popular machines for pulling sidecars.

Linked brakes

Engine doubles as down-tube.

This logo first appeared when P&M adopted the Panther name in 1923.

SPECIFICATIONS
1955 Greeves 20T
- **ENGINE** Villiers 8E two-stroke single
- **CAPACITY** 197cc
- **POWER OUTPUT** 8.4bhp @ 4,000rpm
- **TRANSMISSION** Four-speed, chain drive
- **FRAME** Cast alloy headstock, down-tube, and engine plates
- **SUSPENSION** Rubber-sprung leading-link forks, rear swingarm
- **WEIGHT** 225lb (102kg)
- **TOP SPEED** 55-60mph (88-96km/h)

1955 Greeves 20T

Greeves became famous thanks to its outstanding competition record in trials and scrambling (pp. 152–3). This advanced design incorporated rubber-sprung suspension, a cast-alloy front down-tube, and a Villiers two-stroke power unit.

The steering head and front down-tube are of cast alloy

Leading link forks

Rubber suspension units with friction dampers

Villiers engine

1955 Ariel Square Four

The extraordinary Square Four, often referred to as the "Squariel", has a special place in the history of the Ariel company. Production began in 1930 and continued until the late 1950s. The design used two crankshafts geared together with the two vertical twin-cylinders arranged in a square formation. The 500cc engine was compact and light enough to fit into the frame of a single-cylinder bike. Over the years the design was upgraded and the capacity was increased to 600 and then 1000cc.

Compensated-link rear suspension

"Wedgwood Blue" paintwork

Top yoke mounted speedometer

Single rear-facing carburettor

A four-pipe exhaust design was used from 1954

SPECIFICATIONS

1955 Ariel Square Four
- **ENGINE** Square four-cylinder overhead valve
- **CAPACITY** 997cc
- **POWER OUTPUT** 40bhp @ 5,600rpm
- **TRANSMISSION** Four-speed gearbox, chain drive
- **FRAME** Bolt-up tubular steel cradle
- **SUSPENSION** Telescopic forks, Ariel link and plunger rear
- **WEIGHT** 425lb (193kg)
- **TOP SPEED** 105mph (169km/h)

1963 Ariel Arrow Super Sports

The Ariel Leader, introduced in 1958, was an innovative twin-cylinder two-stroke with a pressed-steel beam frame, trailing link forks, and enclosed bodywork. The Arrow, introduced in 1959, was a more sporting version of the popular Leader design.

Ariel's biggest sellers were the two-stroke twins that appeared in the late fifties when the company was part of the BSA group.

The dummy fuel tank is a storage compartment

Four-speed gearbox

Brake-light switch

The pressed-steel beam frame has a fuel tank under the seat

Trailing link forks

SPECIFICATIONS

1963 Ariel Arrow Super Sports
- **ENGINE** Two-stroke parallel twin
- **CAPACITY** 247cc
- **POWER OUTPUT** 20bhp @ 6500 rpm
- **TRANSMISSION** Four-speed gearbox, chain drive
- **FRAME** Pressed steel beam
- **SUSPENSION** Trailing-link forks, rear swingarm
- **WEIGHT** 285lb (129kg)
- **TOP SPEED** 78mph (125km/h)

Sunbeam's motorcycle club badge

1923 Sunbeam Sprinter

The Sunbeam trademark was first affixed to bicycles at the end of the nineteenth century. From 1913, the company also built motorcycles. Sunbeam's reputation for fine quality and workmanship diminished when the firm was sold in the late 1920s. In 1939, it was sold again to the BSA group; who attached the Sunbeam name to unusual shaft-drive twins. The machine shown below was produced by the original company and was used by the famous Sunbeam rider and record-breaker, George Dance.

Oil and fuel tank

The saddle is spartan as comfort is not a vital quality in a sprint bike

SPECIFICATIONS

1923 Sunbeam Sprinter
- ENGINE Overhead-valve single-cylinder
- CAPACITY 493cc
- POWER OUTPUT 29bhp (estimated)
- TRANSMISSION Three-speed gearbox, chain drive
- FRAME Diamond-pattern frame
- SUSPENSION Sunbeam girder forks
- WEIGHT 240lb (109kg)
- TOP SPEED 78.26mph (126km/h)

Straight-through exhaust

Clutch and exposed primary drive chain

Dummy rim brake

SPECIFICATIONS

1930 Scott TT Replica
- ENGINE Twin-cylinder two-stroke water-cooled
- CAPACITY 596cc
- POWER OUTPUT 24bhp @ 8,000rpm
- TRANSMISSION Albion three-speed gearbox, chain drive
- FRAME Triangulated open tubular (with stressed engine)
- SUSPENSION Telescopic forks
- WEIGHT 335lb (152kg)
- TOP SPEED 90mph (144km/h)

1930 Scott TT Replica

Scott's advanced two-stroke machines were first produced in 1909. Over the next few years they won numerous races, including the Senior TT in 1912 and 1913. After the First World War they never won the race again, although they performed creditably. This production replica was based on the works model that finished third in the 1928 TT.

The wire-mesh guard protects the rider's face from flying stones

The Scott insignia

The triangulated frame was a Scott trademark

Radiator

Undamped telescopic forks

Water-cooled cylinder jacket

Magneto

The lubrication system feeds oil directly to the crankshaft

The removable strap and door allow access to the crankshaft

Graham Walker at the start of the 1929 Ulster GP. His helmet is shown below.

1933 Rudge TT Replica

Rudge won their first TT in 1914 using a machine with an ingenious variable belt drive system. This had been abandoned by the time the first four-valve singles, which were very successful, appeared in 1924. The TT replica was launched in 1931, following the excellent performance by the works bikes in 1930.

The Rudge company logo

SPECIFICATIONS

1933 Rudge TT Replica

- •ENGINE Four-valve overhead single
- •CAPACITY 499cc
- •POWER OUTPUT 32bhp (estimated)
- •TRANSMISSION Four-speed gearbox, chain drive
- •FRAME Open cradle with engine as stressed member
- •SUSPENSION Girder forks
- •WEIGHT 290lb (131kg)
- •TOP SPEED 100mph (160km/h)

Four-valve cylinder head with radial exhaust valves and parallel inlet ports

Friction damper

Heel-and-toe gear pedal

Pushrods operate exposed valvegear

A linked braking system is used

1951 Royal Enfield 500 Twin

Royal Enfield, founded in the 1890s, produced a wide variety of motorcycles. In the late 1940s, following the fashion for parallel twins established by Triumph's Speed Twin (p.74), Enfield built their 500 Twin. All their later parallel twins were based on this design, albeit with greater engine capacities; the last, launched in 1962, had a 736cc engine.

SPECIFICATIONS

1951 Royal Enfield 500

- •ENGINE Overhead-valve parallel twin
- •CAPACITY 495cc
- •POWER OUTPUT 25bhp @ 5,500rpm
- •TRANSMISSION Albion four-speed gearbox, chain drive
- •FRAME Tubular open cradle
- •SUSPENSION Telescopic forks, rear swingarm
- •WEIGHT 390lb (177kg)
- •TOP SPEED 78mph (125.5km/h)

THE ENFIELD BULLET

The Indian army used 350cc Royal Enfield Bullets and production was set up in Madras to supply their needs. Some details were changed, but the overall construction and design remains the same. Indian Bullets, such as this 1992 model, are exported all over the world and even make their way back to Great Britain.

Indicators were not fitted to the original machines

The frame is like that of the Royal Enfield twin below

Knee grips

Distributor ignition

Light switch

The swingarm frame has oil damped suspension

Snail cam-chain adjusters

Oil filler

Italy

Italian motorcycles have always been noted for their inspired design and impressive sporting achievements.

The Moto Guzzi logo

Pioneers, such as Eduardo Bianchi (p.108) and Luigi Fingini, began building motorized two-wheelers around the turn of the century. Frera began production in 1906 and Giuseppe Gilera (pp.96-7) started his business in 1909. Italy took up motorcycles and motorcycle racing with enthusiasm. Famous races were run on public roads, such as the Milano-Napoli, the Giro d'Italia, and the Targa Florio. These races attracted a great following and continued into the fifties and sixties. New firms opened – Benelli (pp.90-91), MM, Garelli (who built their first bike in 1913), and Moto Guzzi (pp.100-03) – but little effort was made to export and competition bikes rarely raced abroad.

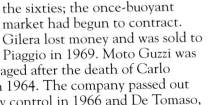

International Racing
Bianchi and Moto Guzzi both went to the Isle of Man for the Tourist Trophy races (pp.152-3) in 1926; Bianchi had little success in the Junior race but Moto Guzzi's excellent 250cc machine won the Lightweight race outright – only to be disqualified for using an unspecified make of spark plug. Nine years later they returned and made no mistakes. Irish rider Stanley Woods won the Senior TT riding a Moto Guzzi. When Mussolini came to power in Italy in 1922, he was eager to see Italian firms succeed in international competition and made money available to support their efforts. Gilera's superb four-cylinder machines, based on Rondine designs, evolved at this time. Dorino Serafini won the 500cc European Championship in 1939 aboard a Gilera, and the company went on to greater achievements after the war.

Fashion on Two Wheels
Reasonably-priced, low-maintenance machines popularized the motorcycle after the Second World War. Road and commuter machines were made in huge quantities, especially by Garelli and Ducati (pp.92-5). Fashion created a demand for scooters. Innocenti and Piaggio, makers of the Lambretta and the Vespa (pp.98-9), arrived on the scene, both of them new to

MV Agusta badge celebrating their 37 World titles

MV Agusta 350 Grand Prix racer

1928 Moto Guzzi 500S

the market. Motorcycle builders MV Agusta (pp.104-07), FB Mondial, and Parilla also started up at this time.

The popularity of small-capacity motorcycles and scooters continued into the fifties and a range of innovative machines were designed and produced during these years.

Claiming the World Championship
When the World Championship was set up in 1949, Italian machines dominated the 125 and 250cc classes. Four-cylinder Gileras and MV Agustas claimed the 500cc title and Moto Guzzi dominated the 350cc class from 1953 until 1957. However, sales declined and the expense of fielding a racing team was considerable. Italian teams, with the exception of MV, pulled out of Grand Prix racing. MV Agusta won every one of the possible 12 world titles between 1958 and 1960. Japanese bikes ended their supremacy, although MV dominated the 500cc class until the mid-seventies.

Surviving the Sixties
Italian industry suffered during the sixties; the once-buoyant market had begun to contract. Gilera lost money and was sold to Piaggio in 1969. Moto Guzzi was mismanaged after the death of Carlo Guzzi in 1964. The company passed out of family control in 1966 and De Tomaso, who also acquired Benelli, took the concern over. In the seventies surviving companies realized that for export success they must concentrate on larger-capacity machines. Guzzi, Ducati, and Laverda (p.109) all became known in foreign markets. Import restrictions protected the home manufacturing base and the Italian industry continued to produce fine motorcycles, while elsewhere, outside Japan, the industry declined. Cagiva swallowed up Ducati, Morini (p.108), and also Sweden's Husqvarna (pp.138-9) in the next decade – while Piaggio become the world's third biggest motorcycle company.

1928 Moto Guzzi

Benelli

THE BENELLI BROTHERS built their first motorcycle in 1921. The factory in Pesaro grew quickly and became known internationally. The early machines were small-capacity two strokes, but in 1927 the firm built a 175cc four-stroke single. This formed the basis for a series of successful racers that were still competing in the 1950s. Financial troubles forced the Benelli family to sell in 1971. New owner Alessandro de Tomaso invested heavily in design development, but Benelli never regained its glory.

Tonino Benelli, the team's star rider, was killed in an accident in 1937, after he had retired from racing.

Australian rider Kel Karruthers won the 1969 250cc World Championship for Benelli on one of the four-cylinder racers that was developed during the sixties. Benelli gained a second world title – Dario Ambrosini had won the 250cc crown in 1950.

1976 Benelli 750 Sei
The 750 Sei was the flagship of the machines commissioned by Alessandro de Tomaso when he took over Benelli in 1971. Based upon Honda's successful four-cylinder machines, the 750 Sei with its additional pair of cylinders, became the world's first six-cylinder production bike. In 1980, a 900cc version was built.

Passenger grab-rail

Seat lock

Three Dell'Orto carburettors feed six cylinders

750 Sei

Be

The Benelli's unique six-pipe exhaust system

The alternator is mounted "piggy back" to reduce engine width

The six Benelli brothers – (from left to right) Tonino, Francesco, Giovanni, Giuseppe, Filippo, and Mino. Giuseppe left to start his own motorcycle company, called "MotoBi", in 1949.

The awkward switchgear is typical of Italian electrical controls of the period

Brake master cylinder

Chrome headlamp. Chrome plating was still used extensively in the seventies

Brake pipe junction

Brembo twin-piston brake callipers

The Honda ancestry of the engine is clear (cf. Honda's CB750 pp.114-5)

Centrally positioned oil filter

Warning lights and essential instruments are housed in the squared-off display pod.

Ball end brake levers

Plug leads

Tappet covers

The engine of the Benelli 750 measures 66cm (26in) across the full width of the crankcase covers.

SPECIFICATIONS

Benelli 750 Sei

- **ENGINE** Overhead-camshaft, in-line six-cylinder single
- **BORE AND STROKE** 56 x 50.6mm(1⅛ x 2in)
- **CAPACITY** 747.77cc
- **POWER OUTPUT** 71bhp @ 8,900rpm
- **CARBURATION** Three 24mm Dell'Orto carbs
- **IGNITION** Battery and coil
- **TRANSMISSION** Five-speed gearbox, chain drive
- **CLUTCH** Wet multiplate
- **FRAME** Tubular steel cradle
- **SUSPENSION** Telescopic forks, rear swingarm
- **BRAKES** Twin front disc brakes, rear drum brakes
- **WEIGHT** 220kg (485lb)
- **TOP SPEED** 190km/h (118mph)
- **YEAR OF CONSTRUCTION** 1976

— DID YOU KNOW? —

The earliest eight-cylinder machine was built by the American aviator and aircraft engine producer, Glenn Curtiss, in 1912. Curtiss, who built single and V-twin motorcycles, fitted an air-cooled V8 aeroplane engine into a motorcycle chassis and used it for record breaking. No road bike has more cylinders than the Benelli 750's Sei.

Ducati

TODAY DUCATI ARE FAMOUS for their sporting motorcycles, but their first machines were bicycles with simple clip-on engines. The crucial event for Ducati's success, was the arrival of designer Fabio Taglioni in 1954. He created a single-cylinder machine, with a shaft-driven overhead camshaft, that formed the basis for the company's range. Taglioni also added Desmodromic valve gear to racing versions (utilizing the camshaft rather than springs to close the valves), this was later adopted on their road bikes. Ducatis became renowned for superb performance and handling.

The first Desmo Ducatis were the very successful 125cc GP bikes of the late 1950s. They were runners-up in the 1958 World Championship.

1964 Ducati 250 Mach 1

Introduced in 1964, the Mach 1 was easily the fastest 250cc road bike available. It greatly enhanced Ducati's growing reputation. Unsurprisingly, many road bikes were converted into racers.

Dell'Orto SS1 carburettor with open bell mouth

Sports-style clip-on handlebars

Points cover

Battery

Heel and toe gear pedal

Alloy wheel rims

SPECIFICATIONS

1964 Ducati 250 Mach 1
- ENGINE Air-cooled overhead-camshaft four-stroke single
- CAPACITY 249cc
- POWER OUTPUT 26bhp @ 8,500rpm
- TRANSMISSION Five-speed gearbox, chain drive
- FRAME Tubular steel cradle
- SUSPENSION Telescopic forks, twin-shock rear swingarm
- WEIGHT 116kg (256lb)
- TOP SPEED 171km/h (106mph)

1974 Ducati 350 Desmo

Desmodromic valve gear became available on Ducati road bikes in 1971, when 250, 350, and 450cc versions of the single were produced with Desmo cylinder heads. The singles had a long production run but grew to be increasingly outdated. Production of these singles finally ceased in 1974. However, Desmodromic valve gear is still a remarkable feature of Ducati machines.

Steering damper

One-piece single seat and tail unit

Rear set linkage

Shaft drive to overhead camshaft

The wide crank-case engine was also available as a 250 and 450cc

SPECIFICATIONS

1974 Ducati 350 Desmo
- ENGINE Air-cooled overhead-camshaft four-stroke single
- CAPACITY 340cc
- POWER OUTPUT 38bhp @ 7,500rpm
- TRANSMISSION Five-speed gearbox, chain drive
- FRAME Tubular steel open cradle
- SUSPENSION Telescopic forks, twin-shock rear swingarm
- WEIGHT 128kg (282lb)
- TOP SPEED 169km/h (105mph)

Clip-on
handlebars

Kickstart
lever

V-twins
have a
slim profile.

Horn

1973 Ducati 750 Sport
*Ducati had been building single-cylinder bikes with shaft-
driven camshafts for fifteen years when they decided to
move into the bigger bike market. The 750cc machine
was effectively two singles mounted in a 90° "V". This
layout became a Ducati trademark. The 750 went on sale
in 1971, and a Sports version appeared the following
year. Later the capacity was increased to 900cc.*

One piece
single-seat
and tail unit

SPECIFICATIONS
1973 Ducati 750 Sport
- **ENGINE** Air-cooled overhead-camshaft
  four-stroke 90° V-twin
- **CAPACITY** 747cc
- **POWER OUTPUT** 55bhp @ 7,900rpm
- **TRANSMISSION** Five-speed, chain drive
- **FRAME** Open cradle with stressed engine
- **SUSPENSION** Telescopic forks,
  twin shock rear swingarm
- **WEIGHT** 181.5kg (400lb)
- **TOP SPEED** 185km/h (115mph)

Ignition
coils

Ignition
points
housing

Oil
sump

Cylinder finning
is longitudinal for
better cooling

Conti
silencers

Lockheed
brake callipers

1989 Ducati 851
*The 851 is the most complex Ducati road bike ever built,
though it still retained Desmodromic valve operation and
the 90° V-twin engine layout. It utilized four camshafts,
eight valves, water cooling, and petrol injection, all firsts
for a road Ducati. The 851 was the basis for the successful
888 Superbike racer.*

Suspension
damping
adjustment
controls

Red is the
Italian racing
colour

Tubular
trellis frame

SPECIFICATIONS
1989 Ducati 851
- **ENGINE** Water-cooled double overhead-
  camshaft eight-valve fuel-injected V-twin
- **CAPACITY** 851cc
- **POWER OUTPUT** 95bhp @ 9000rpm
- **TRANSMISSION** Six-speed gearbox,
  chain drive
- **FRAME** Tubular trellis
- **SUSPENSION** Telescopic anti-
  dive forks, rear swingarm
- **WEIGHT** 180kg (397lb)
- **TOP SPEED** 245km/h (152mph)

Air duct

Valves prevent
the forks from
diving when
braking

Alloy
swingarm

"Floating"
disc brakes

Ducati Imola

COMPETITION SUCCESS HAS always played a vital part in the Ducati legend, and yet it is remarkable how close the similarity is between their racers and road machines. Both are famous for their superb handling and fine performance. Early 125cc Grand Prix machines and the later V-twins were based on production machines; both were very successful. Ducati's decisive win in the 1972 Imola 200 began the successful racing career of their V-twins that continues today with their domination of the World Superbike Championships in the early 1990s.

After 322km (200 miles) only four seconds separated Smart and Spaggiari at the finish of the Imola 200 race.

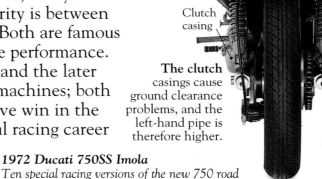

The clutch casings cause ground clearance problems, and the left-hand pipe is therefore higher.

Clutch casing

Glitter flake paint

1972 Ducati 750SS Imola
Ten special racing versions of the new 750 road bike were built to compete in the 1972 Imola 200. Victory would ensure excellent publicity for the racers, and that is exactly what the Ducati team expected to achieve. On the day, Ducati scored a splendid double, with Paul Smart in first place and Bruno Spaggiari second on this bike.

Glass-fibre tail piece

Crankcase breather

Ignition contact switch

Battery (ignition is constant loss)

Threaded block chain adjuster

Centre-stand lugs are still visible on the original road bike frame

Perspex windscreen

The long wheelbase and shallow steering-head angle gives the Ducati exceptional high-speed stability but the steering is heavy.

Oil cooler

A clear band shows the fuel level in the glass fibre tank

Dell'Orto 40mm carbs

Steering damper

The rev counter and oil cooler are housed in the nose of the fairing (as seen above)

Oil cooler air duct

SPECIFICATIONS

Ducati 750 Imola

- •**ENGINE** Overhead-camshaft 90° V-twin, with desmodromic valve operation
- •**BORE AND STROKE** 80 x 74.4mm
- •**CAPACITY** 748cc
- •**POWER OUTPUT** 85bhp @ 8800rpm
- •**CARBURATION** Two 40mm Dell'Orto
- •**IGNITION** 12-volt battery and coil
- •**TRANSMISSION** Five-speed gearbox, chain drive
- •**CLUTCH** Wet multiplate
- •**FRAME** Tubular open cradle with engine as stressed member
- •**SUSPENSION** Telescopic forks, rear swingarm
- •**BRAKES** Twin front discs, single disc rear
- •**WEIGHT** 162kg (356lb)
- •**TOP SPEED** 217km/h (155mph)
- •**YEAR OF CONSTRUCTION** 1972

Alloy wheel rims

Brake caliper bolts are lock-wired together to prevent their becoming loose in use

Oil sump

Leading-axle forks increase fork offset

Gilera

GIUSEPPE GILERA FOUNDED the firm in 1909 when he was only 22 years old. The company grew quickly and, in 1920, moved to the large new factory in Arcore, outside Milan, which they occupy today. Gilera acquired the Rondine design in 1935 and this machine provided the basis for their racers for the next thirty years. The company declined after the early death of Feruccio, Gilera's son, in 1956, and was sold, in 1969, to Piaggio. Best known for the Vespa scooter (p.99) Piaggio also made small two-stroke bikes. New models appeared in 1987 that traded on Gilera's sporting fame. In 1992, Gilera made their return to the Grand Prix arena.

SPECIFICATIONS
1951 Gilera Saturno
- ENGINE Overhead-valve single
- CAPACITY 498cc
- POWER OUTPUT 22bhp @ 5,000rpm
- TRANSMISSION Four-speed gearbox, chain drive
- FRAME Tubular open cradle
- SUSPENSION Girder forks, rear swingarm with parallel springs
- WEIGHT 175kg (386lb)
- TOP SPEED 180km/h (85mph)

Gilera mudguard pennant

Girder forks

1951 Gilera Saturno
The Saturno belonged to a range of Gilera machines made during the forties and fifties. Others included the Mars and Nettuno. The Saturno appeared in 1939, but production only began after the war. This solid sporting bike, based on previous 500cc singles, had few novel features but was attractive and popular; it stayed in the Gilera range until 1959.

Saturno tank transfer

The unit construction engine/gearbox features a large-capacity oil sump

A unique rear-suspension system is controlled by enclosed horizontal springs

1949 Gilera Saturno San Remo
Tuned Saturnos were raced by the factory and a limited number were also made available to customers. In 1947 Carlo Bandirola won at San Remo. Gileras also won for the next four years, and racing versions of the Saturno became known as "San Remos". Although they were raced at international meetings and were a mainstay of Italian national competitions, San Remos never seriously challenged the multi-cylinder or overhead-camshaft machines of the opposition.

35mm Dell'Orto carburettor

Petrol tap

Gearbox linkage

Suspension damper

Alloy wheel rim

Straight-through exhaust

Oil-feed pipe to rockers

1989 Gilera Saturno

- **ENGINE** Single four-stroke four valve
- **CAPACITY** 491cc
- **POWER OUTPUT** 45bhp @ 7,500rpm
- **TRANSMISSION** Five-speed gearbox, chain drive
- **FRAME** Tubular triangulated frame with the engine as a stressed member
- **SUSPENSION** Telescopic forks, rising rate monoshock
- **WEIGHT** 140kg (309lb)
- **TOP SPEED** 185km/h (115mph)

1989 Gilera Saturno

A new Saturno model was built in the late eighties. Originally aimed at the Japanese market, it was eventually sold worldwide. The Nuovo Saturno, like its namesake, is a lightweight, sporting, 500cc single but has all the attributes of a modern machine.

The sculpted fuel tank has a flush filler cap

Half-fairing

Drilled discs

High-level exhaust pipe

Eccentric chain adjuster

Three-spoke alloy wheels

Suspension linkage

Cartridge oil filter

The four-stroke motor is a stressed member of the frame

Blade-type girder forks

SPECIFICATIONS

1949 Gilera Saturno San Remo

- **ENGINE** Overhead-valve, single cylinder four-stroke
- **CAPACITY** 499cc
- **POWER OUTPUT** 38bhp @ 6,000rpm
- **TRANSMISSION** Four-speed gearbox, chain drive
- **FRAME** Tubular steel open cradle
- **SUSPENSION** Girder forks, rear swingarm with horizontal springs
- **WEIGHT** 128kg (282lb)
- **TOP SPEED** 193km/h (120mph)

GILERA'S RACERS

In 1936 Gilera bought the rights to the Rondine racing bike. This advanced four-cylinder machine provided the basis both for Gilera's racers and for the across the frame four-cylinder layout which MV Agusta and the Japanese manufacturers later copied.

A water-cooled, supercharged Gilera four won the European Championship in 1939.

After the war, supercharging was banned and four-cylinder engines were redesigned. Carlo Bandirola (above) rides the 1950 version. Britain's Geoff Duke won the 500cc World Championship on Gileras in 1953, 1954, and 1955.

Gilera won their final championship in 1957 and then retired. Seen above is Gilera team rider Libero Liberati riding a 350cc with a dustbin fairing in 1957.

Scooters

THE SCOOTER FIRST BECAME popular between 1916 and 1924 when a number of curious machines were produced. The concept of an easy-to-ride, small-wheeled bike was revived during the Second World War when folding machines were designed to be dropped by parachute for the use of airmen. Cheap transport was needed after the war, and skills that had been employed in the manufacture of armaments were diverted into motorcycle and scooter production. Offering some weather protection and enough power to keep up with town traffic, the economical scooter had its heyday in the fifties and sixties as commuter and leisure transport.

NSU built Lambretta scooters under licence before developing their own machines.

The Lambretta engine and gearbox unit is pivoted to provide rear suspension.

Engine and gearbox unit forms part of the rear suspension

1957 Lambretta LD150
Lambrettas were first built in 1947, and in 1951 legshields and engine covers were offered as an optional feature, although they later became standard fittings. The LD model sold in vast numbers until it was discontinued in 1959. Production of Lambrettas ceased in Italy in the 1970s but continued under licence in Spain and India.

Many scooters carry a spare wheel

Handlebar end mirror

Most scooters used a twist-grip gear change

THE AUTOPED

The versatile American-made Autoped was produced in 1915 and built under licence in England and Germany. It fitted neatly into the boot of a car.

The handlebars folded flat for storage

Handlebars were pushed forward to engage drive

155cc motor

The seatless Autoped was designed to be driven standing up!

SPECIFICATIONS

1957 Lambretta LD150
- **ENGINE** Fan-cooled two stroke
- **CAPACITY** 148cc
- **POWER OUTPUT** 8bhp
- **TRANSMISSION** Three-speed hand-change gearbox, shaft drive
- **FRAME** Pressed-steel monocoque construction
- **SUSPENSION** Single-sided trailing-link forks, rear drive housing acts as swingarm
- **WEIGHT** 75kg (165lb)
- **TOP SPEED** 80.5km/h (50mph)

Easily removable covers protect the engine and gearbox unit from weather and crash damage.

All-enclosing bodywork

The trailing-link forks used rubber springs

SPECIFICATIONS

1956 Heinkel Tourist

- **ENGINE** Overhead-valve single-cylinder
- **CAPACITY** 174cc
- **POWER OUTPUT** 9.5bhp @ 5,500rpm
- **TRANSMISSION** Four-speed gearbox, chain drive
- **FRAME** Pressed-steel spine
- **SUSPENSION** Telescopic forks (with external damper), and rear pivoted engine unit
- **WEIGHT** 145kg (320lb)
- **TOP SPEED** 95km/h (59mph)

1956 Heinkel Tourist

Heinkel were famous German aircraft manufacturers, but after the Second World War the building of aeroplanes was restricted in Germany and Heinkel used their expertise to produce scooters. The high-quality 149cc Tourist scooter was introduced in 1953 and was followed by other machines including bubble cars. Aircraft production restarted in the fifties and in 1965 scooter production ceased.

Heinkel built 100,000 Tourists.

The Heinkel has an unusual faired-in front wheel.

Fold-down luggage rack

Helmet lock

Indicators

Spare wheel

Overhead-valve four-stroke engine

Shock absorber lower mounting

Engine inspection flap

The 1960s "Mods" cult occurred in England in the 1960s. Mods rode customized scooters and clashed with motorcycle "Rocker" gangs at English coastal resorts.

SPECIFICATIONS

1963 Vespa GS160 Mk I

- **ENGINE** Single-cylinder fan-cooled two stroke
- **CAPACITY** 159cc
- **POWER OUTPUT** 8bhp @ 6,500rpm
- **TRANSMISSION** Four-speed, direct drive
- **FRAME** Pressed-steel monocoque construction
- **SUSPENSION** Single-sided trailing-link forks and rear pivoted engine unit
- **WEIGHT** 110kg (242lb)
- **TOP SPEED** 100km/h (62mph)

1963 Vespa Grand Sport 160 Mark 1

The Vespa (which means "wasp" in Italian) has evolved steadily since 1947. The original concept was excellent and has stood the test of time. The monocoque chassis, the engine, and gearbox unit still follow the layout of the early machines.

Clutch and gearchange

The GS is regarded by many as the best Vespa ever built.

Horn cover

Single-sided front fork

Spare wheel

The waisted rear of the GS made it one of best-looking scooters marketed in the sixties.

Choke

Petrol tap

Foot brake

The engine is mounted on the right

Moto Guzzi

Foundations for the Moto Guzzi company were laid before the First World War by Italian Air Force pilots Giovanni Ravelli and Giorgio Parodi, and Carlo Guzzi, their mechanic and driver. Ravelli was killed in the war but Guzzi and Parodi went on to set up the company at Mandello del Lario. Their first prototype, designed by Guzzi, was built in 1920. It was an advanced four-valve overhead-camshaft horizontal single-cylinder machine. A more conventional two-valve layout was adopted for production. Excellent design, quality construction, and high performance made Moto Guzzi one of Italy's biggest manufacturers.

Carlo Guzzi (above) gave his name to the company, although he and Giorgio Parodi were partners. Guzzi died in 1964, aged 75.

Gear lever

Valve lifter

Oil tank

Air filter

1928 Moto Guzzi 500S
The 498.4cc Moto Guzzi had one of the longest production runs of any motorcycle. The 1920 model was so advanced in its design that the last Guzzi single, built in 1976, had the same bore and stroke dimensions of the original. The S model with its hand gear-change and rigid rear end was one of the most basic versions.

A front view of the 500S reveals the pleasing symmetry of its layout.

Luggage rack

The tool tray is recessed into the fuel tank

Oil pump / Valve-lifter releases compression

The famous "bacon slicer" flywheel was a notable feature of Moto Guzzi's big single-cylinder machines until the late sixties. This engine was also used to power a popular three-wheeled truck.

Girder forks with central springs

Drum brake

The chrome wheel rims are not an original feature

"Bacon slicer" external flywheel

Kick starter

Choke and ignition controls

Inverted brake lever

MOTO GUZZI

The Eagle motif was used by the Italian Air Force, it was chosen by Guzzi and Parodi as a logo in tribute to their friend Giovanni Ravelli, who died in action.

The oil tank is set across the frame

Hairpin valve spring

The overhead exhaust valve is positioned to receive optimum cooling

A side-valve controls the inlet port

SPECIFICATIONS

Moto Guzzi 500S

- **ENGINE** Inlet-over-exhaust horizontal single
- **BORE AND STROKE** 88 x 82mm (3½ x 3¼in)
- **CAPACITY** 498.4cc
- **POWER OUTPUT** 18bhp @ 4,000rpm
- **CARBURATION** Amac carburettors
- **IGNITION** Coil
- **TRANSMISSION** Three-speed handchange gearbox, chain drive
- **CLUTCH** Wet multiplate
- **FRAME** Tubular open steel cradle with sheet steel engine plates
- **SUSPENSION** Girder forks, rigid rear
- **BRAKES** Drum brakes, front and rear
- **WEIGHT** 130kg (287lb)
- **TOP SPEED** 100km/h (62mph)
- **YEAR OF CONSTRUCTION** 1928

Post-war Moto Guzzis

Moto Guzzi are not afraid to stick with good ideas – their excellent flat-single design lasted fifty years before it was declared obsolete. A new design began production in 1967, and it has been the mainstay of the Guzzi range ever since. The shaft-driven 90° V-twin was originally intended for police and military use, but was subsequently developed as a tourer and later as a sports bike.

SPECIFICATIONS

1946 Moto Guzzi Dondolino
- **ENGINE** Overhead-valve single
- **CAPACITY** 498.4cc
- **POWER OUTPUT** 33bhp @ 5,500rpm
- **TRANSMISSION** Four-speed gearbox, chain drive
- **FRAME** Tube and plate with stressed engine
- **SUSPENSION** Girder forks, rear swingarm with springs under engine
- **WEIGHT** 128kg (282lb)
- **TOP SPEED** 170km/h (106mph)

1946 Moto Guzzi Dondolino

The Dondolino (meaning "rocking chair") was a production racer built from 1946 to 1951. The single-cylinder Moto Guzzis were very successfully raced by the factory and by independent racers.

The oil tank is located on top of the fuel tank

Centrally sprung girder forks

Large diameter drum brake with internal actuating arm

Second duct at rear of drum to allow greater air flow

Hairpin valve springs

The rear suspension springs are mounted under the engine

MOTO GUZZI'S RACERS

Although conservative in their approach to the development of road bikes, Moto Guzzi's designers produced some remarkable racing machines.

These included supercharged three-cylinders, in-line shaft-driven fours, 120° V-twins and the amazing 500cc V8 that made its debut in 1954.

MOTO GUZZI V8

The V8 was designed by the famous Moto Guzzi designer, Guilo Carcano. In 1957 a V8 machine achieved 243km/h

(151mph) over 10km (6¼ miles) from a standing start in 1957 but Guzzi withdrew from racing later that year, with the potential of the V8 engine unrealized.

Works rider Bill Lomas shows how lightweight the V8 power unit is.

The original seats were uncomfortable and were replaced with this new improved design

Ignition coils

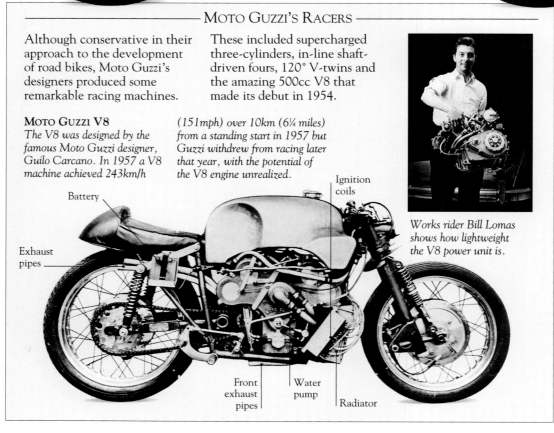

Battery

Exhaust pipes

Front exhaust pipes

Water pump

Radiator

- ENGINE Overhead-valve transverse V-twin
- CAPACITY 757cc
- POWER OUTPUT 40bhp @ 5,000rpm
- TRANSMISSION Four-speed gearbox, shaft drive
- FRAME Tubular steel cradle with leading axle forks
- SUSPENSION Telescopic forks, rear swingarm
- WEIGHT 234kg (516lb)
- TOP SPEED 180km/h (112mph)

1970 Moto Guzzi V7 Special

Moto Guzzi's first V7s used a 704cc engine but, in 1969, the capacity was increased to 757cc and a few other small changes were made. The improved machine was called the V7 Special, and closely followed the style of its predecessor.

The screen is an American market option

Crash bars

Valanced mudguards

Slatted side panel hides air filter

Right foot gearchange

Cylinder protectors

1976 Moto Guzzi 850 Le Mans Mark1

The introduction of a new, better handling chassis in 1972 brought a change in character for the V-twin. The first sporting 750s were followed in 1976 by a long line of Le Mans models.

Short and streamlined bikini fairing

Non-standard air filters

Cast alloy wheels

Horn

Linked brakes are operated by foot pedal. The second front disc is controlled by the handlebar lever

The lower frame rails unbolt for easy engine removal

Drilled discs assist heat and water dispersal

SPECIFICATIONS

1976 Moto Guzzi Le Mans
- ENGINE Overhead-valve V-twin
- CAPACITY 844cc
- POWER OUTPUT 71bhp @ 7,300rpm
- TRANSMISSION Five-speed gearbox, shaft drive
- FRAME Tubular steel cradle
- SUSPENSION Telescopic forks, rear swingarm
- WEIGHT 216kg (476lb)
- TOP SPEED 212km/h (132mph)

MV Agusta 350

THE LEGEND OF MV AGUSTA is based on phenomenal racing success. From their debut, in 1950, to 1976, when the challenge from Japanese two strokes proved to be too powerful, MV Agusta won 37 World Championships and 273 Grand Prix. In 1958, 1959, and 1960, they won every solo championship. MV Agusta won their last world title in 1974, and their last Grand Prix in Germany in the 1976 season.

John Surtees, MV Agusta's most successful rider of the 1950s, won seven championships for the team. Here he is about to start the 1956 Isle of Man Junior TT.

Brake air scoops

Factory race bikes evolve year by year. The MV 350's frame (seen from the front, above) was first used in the 1960 season, but the engine was used from 1954 to 1961.

Oil feed for gearbox sprocket outrigger bearing

MV 350cc Works Grand Prix
MV's first Grand Prix bikes were single cylinder 125cc and 500cc fours. The 350cc version of the four was built in 1953, but did not achieve a notable success until 1958, when it won the first of four successive World Championships.

Box section swingarm

The chain adjustment is by eccentrics on a spindle

The frame unbolts at this point to allow the engine to be removed easily

Two camshaft covers dominate the engine of the MV Agusta (seen here without its fairing). The clutch lever is angled upwards to make the rider more comfortable when in a prone position for racing.

The engine casings are made of magnesium alloy

Steering damper

The MV logo stands for Meccanica Verghera. The wings and gear signify Agusta's aeronautical connection, and commitment to engineering excellence

Ventilated twin drum-brakes with air-scoops both sides

SPECIFICATIONS

MV Agusta Works 350

- •ENGINE Double overhead-camshaft four-cylinder works racer engine
- •BORE AND STROKE 47.5 x 47mm
- •CAPACITY 347cc
- •POWER OUTPUT 42bhp @ 11,000rpm
- •CARBURATION 4 x Dell'Orto SS1
- •IGNITION Magneto
- •TRANSMISSION Five-speed gearbox, chain drive
- •CLUTCH Wet multiplate
- •FRAME Tubular steel cradle with bolt-up lower rails
- •SUSPENSION Telescopic forks, rear swingarm
- •BRAKES Four leading-shoe front drum brake with single leading shoe rear drum brake
- •WEIGHT 145kg (320lb)
- •TOP SPEED 210km/h (130mph)
- •YEAR OF CONSTRUCTION As these factory racers were never mass-produced, parts of varying ages were combined in each bike.

The blue background for the racing number indicates a 350cc class machine

The alloy fairing bears scars from hard cornering

MV Agusta

THE PRIMARY BUSINESS of the MV Agusta group was, and still is, the manufacture of aircraft. Motorcycle production only began after the Second World War, but continued for thirty years. Bikes in production ranged from scooters to superbikes, as well as the famous racers. When profits from motorcycles vanished in the 1970s, Agusta turned again to aircraft.

The legendary Mike Hailwood making his racing debut on a 250cc MV Agusta.

Hailwood's MV team helmet

SPECIFICATIONS
1953 MV Agusta 125
- **ENGINE** Single overhead-camshaft four-stroke single
- **CAPACITY** 123.5cc
- **POWER OUTPUT** 14bhp @ 10,000rpm
- **TRANSMISSION** Four-speed gearbox, chain drive
- **FRAME** Duplex cradle
- **SUSPENSION** Telescopic forks, rear swingarm
- **WEIGHT** 75kg (165lb)
- **TOP SPEED** 160km/h (100mph)

1953 MV Agusta 125
As well as their own phenomenally successful works racers MV built production racers for the smaller capacity classes. These achieved considerable success in the hands of amateur riders throughout the 1950s. No four-cylinder racers were ever sold.

The fuel tank has been sculpted to accommodate the rider's knees

At the front, suspension is by central spring, with damping in the "legs".

The mudguard stays are drilled for lightness

The brake drum material is magnesium alloy

Dell'Orto carb with remote float bowl

Gear-drive case for the overhead camshaft

Duplex cradle frame

SPECIFICATIONS
1956 MV Agusta 175CS
- **ENGINE** Overhead-camshaft single cylinder
- **CAPACITY** 174cc
- **POWER OUTPUT** 11bhp @ 6,700rpm
- **TRANSMISSION** Four-speed gearbox, chain drive
- **FRAME** Tubular cradle, with engine as stressed member
- **SUSPENSION** Earles forks, rear swingarm
- **WEIGHT** 110kg (242lb)
- **TOP SPEED** 115km/h (71mph)

1956 MV Agusta 175CS Disco Volante
The 175CS was simply put together but the machine looked handsome and had a fine pedigree. Its nickname, "Flying Saucer", was derived from the fuel tank's shape (seen clearly from the front).

Typical of MV's small-capacity road bikes, the 175CS was a popular machine.

Earles forks

Flying-saucer-shaped fuel tank

The banana-shaped frame sections are metal castings

Heel and toe gear lever

The open cradle frame uses the engine as a stressed member

1968 MV Agusta 600
- **ENGINE** Double overhead-camshaft four cylinder
- **CAPACITY** 591.8cc
- **POWER OUTPUT** 52bhp @ 8,200rpm
- **TRANSMISSION** Five-speed gearbox, shaft drive
- **FRAME** Tubular steel cradle
- **SUSPENSION** Telescopic forks, rear swingarm
- **WEIGHT** 221kg (487lb)
- **TOP SPEED** 160km/h (100mph)

1968 MV Agusta 600

MV Agusta built a prototype four-cylinder road bike as early as 1950, although a production version was not marketed until 1966. In view of MV's racing success, it is surprising that their first four-cylinder road bike was a shaft-driven tourer, but production continued until 1971 when a sports 750 was finally introduced. Four-cylinder MVs were all very expensive.

The front view of the MV Agusta 600 is dominated by its Fiat car headlight.

Two independently operated horns of different volumes are fitted

Bar end indicators

Centrally mounted distributor

Twin carbs intake with bell mouths

Cable-operated discs

Belt-driven dynamo is under gearbox

The tank logo celebrates an impressive 37 Road-racing World Championship titles for MV.

1975 MV Agusta 750S America

This revised version of the 750 was introduced in 1975 and intended for the potentially lucrative American market. Unfortunately sales were poor and many of the machines were eventually sold in other countries. Production of the fours ceased in 1977.

Suede-covered seat

The American market required quieter exhausts

1975 MV Agusta 750S America
- **ENGINE** Double overhead-camshaft in-line four cylinder
- **CAPACITY** 789cc
- **POWER OUTPUT** 75bhp @ 8,500rpm
- **TRANSMISSION** Five-speed gearbox, shaft drive
- **FRAME** Duplex cradle
- **SUSPENSION** Telescopic forks, rear swingarm
- **WEIGHT** 240kg (529lb)
- **TOP SPEED** 210km/h (130mph)

Alloy wheel rims

Shaft drive

Four 26mm carbs

Twin disc brakes

Other Classics

1937 Bianchi ES250/1

Eduardo Bianchi was a bicycle and motorcycle pioneer who started building pedal cycles in the 1880s. He first attached an engine to one of his bicycles before the turn of the century, becoming Italy's first motor-cycle manufacturer. Bianchi grew rapidly, branching out into building aeroplane engines, cars, and trucks. After the war the company struggled to compete with other manufacturers. Motorcycle production ceased in 1967, though bicycles bearing the famous name are still built.

SPECIFICATIONS

1937 Bianchi ES250/1
• ENGINE Overhead-camshaft single
• CAPACITY 248cc
• POWER OUTPUT 10bhp @ 4,800rpm
• TRANSMISSION Four-speed gearbox, chain drive
• FRAME Open cradle with engine as stressed member
  • SUSPENSION Girder forks, plunger springing at rear
  • WEIGHT 148kg (326lb)
  • TOP SPEED 105km/h (65mph)

Sky-blue paint was also used on Bianchi bicycles

Petrol cap retaining-clip

Exposed valve springs

Pressed-steel girder forks

Gear-driven magneto

Shaft drive for overhead camshaft

Oil cooling is enhanced because the tank is in front of the engine

SPECIFICATIONS

1974 Moto Morini 3½
• ENGINE Overhead-valve V-twin
• CAPACITY 344cc
• POWER OUTPUT 39bhp @ 8,500rpm
• TRANSMISSION Six-speed gearbox, chain drive
• FRAME Tubular steel cradle
• SUSPENSION Telescopic forks, rear swingarm
• WEIGHT 154kg (340lb)
• TOP SPEED 161km/h (100mph)

1974 Morini 3½ Sport

Morini have a reputation for the effective development of simple designs; their 250cc single cylinder racer almost beat the mighty Honda four in the 1963 World Championship. The 350cc V-twin was introduced in 1972 and was available in Sport and Strada versions; 250 and 500cc machines were also built. Morini are now part of the Cagiva group.

SPECIFICATIONS

1992 Bimota Tesi 1D
• ENGINE Desmodromic two-cylinder four-stroke 90° V-twin
• CAPACITY 904cc
• POWER OUTPUT 118bhp @ 9,000rpm
• TRANSMISSION Six-speed gearbox, chain drive
• FRAME Aluminium alloy frame sections with stressed engine
• SUSPENSION Front and rear swingarms
• WEIGHT 188kg (414lb)
• TOP SPEED 266km/h (165mph)

Chrome headlight

Clip-on handlebars

Stainless steel mudguards

Sport seat

Flanged alloy wheel rims

Ventilated double-sided drum brake

Unique 72° V-twin engine

Heron cylinder head design

SPECIFICATIONS

1982 Laverda Jota 180
- **ENGINE** Double overhead camshaft triple
- **CAPACITY** 920cc
- **POWER OUTPUT** 90bhp @ 8,000rpm
- **TRANSMISSION** Five-speed gearbox, chain drive
- **FRAME** Tubular cradle
- **SUSPENSION** Telescopic forks, rear swingarm
- **WEIGHT** 236kg (520lb)
- **TOP SPEED** 224km/h (139mph)

1982 Laverda Jota 180

The fastest production motorcycle available in the late 1970s was the Laverda Jota; a tuned version of Laverda's 1000cc triple. The Jota was a triumph of brute force over finesse: it was noisy, heavy, and vibrated; production did not continue for long in the ecologically-aware eighties.

The Laverda factory also produced a range of agricultural machinery. The company retained the same logo.

Laverda's Jota was one of the last unfaired sports bikes.

Orange became the favourite colour for Laverdas

Adjustable handlebars

Oil cooler

Twin Brembo disc brakes

Jota specification silencers

Camshaft chain tensioner

Alternator cover

1992 Bimota Tesi 1D

Bimota are specialist motorcycle builders who make about 300 hand-finished machines per year, designed to house engines made by other makers. Exclusive design and labour-intensive construction techniques make these bikes very expensive. The Tesi was the first production machine to use hub-centre steering.

Total enclosure bodywork

Radiator duct

Innovative hub-centre steering replaces conventional telescopic forks to achieve superior handling.

Flush-fitting fuel cap

Radiator

Shock absorber pivot

Eight-valve Ducati engine

Alloy frame plates

Steering linkage

Swingarm restricts steering lock

Japan

From a modest beginning, Japan has grown to become the world's biggest motorcycle producer in less than fifteen years.

Motorcycles have been built in Japan since 1909 when Miyata built prototype machines. European and American bikes were imported; Harley-Davidsons were built under licence for ten years although, by 1935, Japanese components were being used in their construction. Only after the Second World War were the foundations of a Japanese industry laid. The devastation caused by the war left Japan in chaos financially. Public transport was erratic and private vehicles were not available. The demand for cheap personal transport prompted new companies, such as Honda (pp.112-7), to spring up, and the existing ones saw potential for profit in motorcycles. Early machines were small, simple-to-ride, cheap, and had no sporting pretensions.

The early Kawasaki logo

The Big Four
An economic slump put many makers out of business in the mid-fifties, after the Korean War. Honda emerged as the biggest manufacturer, with Suzuki (pp.124-7) and Yamaha (pp.128-31) established as major producers. Kawasaki (pp.120-23), the smallest of the "big four" did not build bikes in large numbers until 1961. Small firms such as Bridgestone, Lilac, Tohatsu, Marusho, and Meguro became successful. Camera specialists Olympus, and radio makers Sanyo, also dabbled in the bike market.

New Markets
Honda began to export bikes in 1959. Suzuki, Yamaha, and Kawasaki soon followed. Japanese companies had competed fiercely in the home market, developing new machines, new production techniques, and new marketing strategies while

British makers, then the most successful in the world, rested on their laurels. By 1961, Honda were the biggest motorcycle manufacturing company in the world. Japanese motorcycles were clean, reliable, and good fun to ride. If the bike designs were not innovative, the high quality and durability of equipment provided were a revelation to Western riders. Overhead-camshaft engines, electric starters, indicators, and five-speed gearboxes, were not new features, but Japanese machines carried them all as standard fittings, even on 125cc machines.

1979 Kawasaki KR750

1992 Honda Gold Wing

Entering the Race Arena
Honda made their first race appearance at the 1959 Isle of Man Tourist Trophy meeting (pp.152-3). Their reliable but slow bikes won the manufacturers' team prize in the 125cc class. Faster machines were designed for the following year and, in 1961, their works team took the first five places in the 125 and 250cc races, as well as the World Championships in both these categories. Following Honda's race successes, Suzuki, Yamaha, and later Kawasaki, took turns to dominate the racetracks of the world.

Bigger and Better
British manufacturers clung the "big bike" market, believing themselves invincible in this area. However Honda's CB750 in 1968 (p.114) brought a turning point in the history of motorcycling. As fast as the finest machines on the market, if not faster, the CB750 also offered a degree of sophistication that eclipsed its rivals. Honda's spectacular entry into the big bike market was soon followed by Kawasaki, Suzuki, and Yamaha. For over three decades, the Japanese industry has been unquestionably the world's biggest, geared towards providing motorcycles for every market niche.

1971 Suzuki GT750

1960 Honda Benly

Honda

HONDA'S FIRST MOTORIZED bicycle was such a success, that by the mid 1950s they lead the home market. In 1959, they sent their first factory team to the Isle of Man T.T. races; though unsuccessful initially, by 1961 Hondas were good enough to win 125 and 250cc T.T.s. Honda were quick to adapt to the Western market: by the mid-1960s, they dominated world sales.

Born in 1906, the son of a blacksmith, Soichiro Honda founded Honda Motors in 1948. He died in 1992.

1958 Honda C100 Super Cub
Introduced in 1958, the Cub was originally designed as basic, cheap transport. It subsequently became the biggest selling motorcycle ever made, in fact such was its success that derivatives are still being produced.

Plastic legshields

Air filter

Leading-link forks

Choke lever

Enclosed chain

SPECIFICATIONS
1958 Honda C100 Super Cub
- **ENGINE** Overhead-valve horizontal single
- **CAPACITY** 49cc
- **POWER OUTPUT** 4.5bhp @ 9,500rpm
- **TRANSMISSION** Three speed gearbox, automatic clutch, chain drive
- **FRAME** Pressed steel
- **SUSPENSION** Leading-link forks, rear swingarm
- **WEIGHT** 64.9kg (143lb)
- **TOP SPEED** 69.6km/h (42mph)

Four carburettors

Rev counter

Twin-camshaft sixteen-valve engine

The first 250cc Honda four, appeared in Europe in 1960. It went on to win the World Championships in 1961, 1962, and 1963. Here Australian rider Tom Phillis rides to victory in the 1961 French Grand Prix.

1959 Honda RC160
Honda's first four-cylinder machine was built to compete in the All Japan Championships of 1959. It did not compete in the T.T. races that year, but the design was revised and taken to Europe the following season. In 1961 Mike Hailwood won the 250cc World Championship for Honda on an RC 162.

SPECIFICATIONS
1959 Honda RC160
- **ENGINE** Double overhead-camshaft, in-line four cylinder
- **CAPACITY** 249cc
- **POWER OUTPUT** 35bhp @ 14,000rpm
- **TRANSMISSION** Five-speed, chain drive
- **FRAME** Tubular spine
- **SUSPENSION** Leading-link fork, rear swingarm
- **WEIGHT** 124kg (273lb)
- **TOP SPEED** 201km/h (125mph)

Spine frame uses the engine as a stressed member

Ignition coils

Alloy fairing

1967 Honda CB72 Dream

Typical of the style of the early Hondas, the Dream uses a pressed steel spine and leading-link forks. These components would soon be confined to commuter machines, as Honda adopted conventional telescopic forks and tubular frames. This model's name was a particular favourite with Soichiro Honda.

Knee grips on the side of the petrol tank

Instruments mounted in headlight

Single carburettor hidden behind cowling

Pressed steel frame

Pressed steel leading-link forks

The chain's life is prolonged by being enclosed

Electric start is mounted in front of the crankshaft

SPECIFICATIONS

1967 Honda CB72 Dream
- **ENGINE** Overhead camshaft parallel twin
- **CAPACITY** 250cc
- **POWER OUTPUT** 23bhp @ 8500rpm
- **TRANSMISSION** Four-speed gearbox, chain drive
- **FRAME** Pressed steel frame, engine as stressed member
- **SUSPENSION** Leading-link forks, rear swingarm
- **WEIGHT** 152kg (336lb)
- **TOP SPEED** 156km/h (97mph)

1966 Honda CB77 Super Hawk

The CB77 produced maximum power at 9,000rpm, which was unheard of for road bikes in the early sixties – except on other Hondas. The Super Hawk also handled, stopped, and stayed together better than almost any other bike in its class. This bike overcame Western prejudice, by proving that the Japanese could build big, good-looking, high-powered machines.

Tubular-spine frame uses engine as stressed member

Twin carburettors

Combined speedometer and rev counter

Twin leading-shoe, rear drum brake

Foot rest position is adjustable

Unusual forward-push kickstarter

Electric starter

Leading-link forks with suspension units in the legs

Honda advertising presented a clean, fun image of motorcycling in the sixties.

SPECIFICATIONS

1966 Honda CB77 Super Hawk
- **ENGINE** Overhead-camshaft two-cylinder
- **CAPACITY** 305cc
- **POWER OUTPUT** 27.4bhp @ 9000rpm
- **TRANSMISSION** Four-speed gearbox, chain drive
- **FRAME** Tubular backbone
- **SUSPENSION** Telescopic forks, rear swingarm
- **WEIGHT** 160kg (353lb)
- **TOP SPEED** 166km/h (103mph)

Honda

H AVING CONCENTRATED THEIR early efforts on small machines – leaving big motorcycles to established manufacturers in Britain, America, and Europe – Honda introduced the CB750 in 1968. This bike represents a logical progression of Honda's design philosophy, as they moved into the big bike class. The CB750 established a benchmark of fine performance, reliability, and sophistication at an affordable price. It was not surpassed until Kawasaki produced the Z1 (p.120-21) in 1973.

A single wing is the Honda logo.

1969 Honda CB750

With the CB750, Honda made four-cylinder motorcycling available at a realistic price and established disc brakes, five-speed gearboxes, and electric starters as essential features of a modern superbike. Despite criticisms of the CB750's weight and handling, it was a huge success. The design was later scaled down to produce four-cylinder bikes as small as a 350cc.

A flamboyant set of four exhaust pipes suggests impressive speed and power

Oil filler cap

Dry sump oil tank (rare in a Japanese motorcycle)

Cam chain tensioner

Single overhead cam engine

1980 Honda CBX1000

Although the CB750's across-the-frame four had established Honda in the big bike market, they waited ten years before introducing an across-the-frame six-cylinder machine. This time the combination was too much for public taste and despite its superb engine and looks the CBX never won favour.

The engine is suspended from a tubular spine frame

SPECIFICATIONS

1980 Honda CBX1000
- ENGINE Double overhead-camshaft, in-line six cylinder
- CAPACITY 1047cc
- POWER OUTPUT 105bhp @ 9,000rpm
- TRANSMISSION Five-speed, chain drive
- FRAME Tubular spine
- SUSPENSION Telescopic forks, rear swingarm
- WEIGHT 252kg (556lb)
- TOP SPEED 217km/h (135mph)

Ventilated twin discs

Comstar wheels

Oil cooler

1969 Honda CB750

- **ENGINE** Single ohc in-line four
- **CAPACITY** 736cc
- **POWER OUTPUT** 67bhp @ 8,000rpm
- **TRANSMISSION** Five-speed, chain drive
- **FRAME** Tubular cradle
- **SUSPENSION** Telescopic front forks, rear swingarm, twin shock
- **WEIGHT** 220kg (485lb)
- **TOP SPEED** 199km/h (123.5mph)

THE MOTORCYCLE OF THE FUTURE

The NR750 is simply the most complex and expensive production motorcycle ever built. Using advanced technology and exotic materials, Honda have produced an extravagant machine that is not only a magnificent motorcycle, but also a corporate statement of their power in the marketplace.

The NR750's oval pistons each have two conrods

Aerodynamic fairing

Air duct

The bodywork is made of carbon fibre

Upside-down forks

Single-sided swingarm

The CB750 was the first production machine fitted with a disc brake

"Fast Freddie" Spencer won a great many Grand Prix (pp.144-7) 500cc titles for Honda in 1985.

1984 Honda RS500

- **ENGINE** Reed-valve 90° V3 water-cooled two-stroke
- **CAPACITY** 499cc
- **POWER OUTPUT** 130bhp @ 11,500rpm
- **TRANSMISSION** Six-speed, chain drive
- **FRAME** Box-section alloy duplex cradle
- **SUSPENSION** Anti-dive telescopic forks, rear swingarm with single shock
- **WEIGHT** 120kg (264.5lb) (estimated)
- **TOP SPEED** 282km/h (175mph)

One exhaust exits at the rider's right foot, two more exit at the rear of the seat hump

Steering damper

Fuel tank breather valve

Alloy frame

1984 Honda RS500

Honda always preferred four-stroke engines to two strokes. They made their Grand Prix comeback in 1979 with a four-stroke engine, however, they went on to win the 1983 championship with a superb two-stroke machine.

Lightweight racing-type Comstar wheels

Box-section swingarm

115

Honda Gold Wing

THE SYMBOL OF THE GOLDEN WING was already a familiar Honda trademark when the model was christened in 1975. At the time of its launch, the 1000cc four-cylinder machine was simply the biggest, most complex motorcycle ever produced in Japan. By the 1980s, Honda were established motorcar makers, with car and motorcycle assembly plants around the world. In 1981, Gold Wing production moved from Japan to Ohio; the biggest market for the bike was in America, but it was exported all over the world, including Japan. A new 1520cc, six-cylinder Gold Wing – the largest, most complex bike ever built in the USA – was unveiled in 1988.

Storage compartments

A rear view of the massive Gold Wing.

1991 Honda GL1500/6 Gold Wing
Developed from the original flat four, the state-of-the-art Gold Wing has an extra pair of cylinders and 1500cc. This machine inspires either love or hate: for some people, the Gold Wing is the ultimate two-wheeled luxury motorcycle, for others it is an overweight, ugly, and expensive monolith. The example shown here is the 500,000th Honda to be built in America.

Radio aerial mounting position

The large top box has a removable luggage bag

Two helmet locks are fitted

Panniers are removable for rear-wheel access

— DID YOU KNOW? —
Worldwide membership of the international Gold Wing Owners' Clubs exceeds 65,000 registered riders.

The bike is fitted with cast alloy wheels as standard

Digital clock and radio-frequency indicator

Loud-speakers

Air pressure control for rear suspension

Fuel filler flap

Reverse lever

1975 HONDA GOLD WING

The original Gold Wing was supplied without factory-fitted panniers or fairing. Many Gold Wings were modified for long-distance touring by their owners, prompting Honda to start equipping later models with these accessories as standard.

Dummy fuel tank, the real one is under the seat

Twin front disc brakes

1000cc flat-four engine

The handlebar lever operates an additional front brake

Radio/cassette player

The windscreen adjusts to suit the rider

Air vents for radiator cooling

SPECIFICATIONS

Honda GL1500/6 Gold Wing
- **ENGINE** Overhead camshaft, water-cooled, horizontally opposed flat six
- **BORE AND STROKE** 71 x 64mm
- **CAPACITY** 1520cc
- **POWER OUTPUT** 100bhp @ 5,200rpm
- **CARBURATION** Two 33mm C.V.
- **IGNITION** Electronic
- **TRANSMISSION** Five forward speeds with electric reverse, shaft drive
- **CLUTCH** Hydraulically operated wet multiplate
- **FRAME** Dual down-pipe cradle
- **SUSPENSION** Telescopic forks, rear swingarm
- **BRAKES** Twin discs front, rear disc with linked operation
- **WEIGHT** 368kg (811lb)
- **TOP SPEED** 187km/h (116mph)
- **YEAR OF CONSTRUCTION** 1991

Linked front and rear brakes are operated by the foot pedal

Flat six water-cooled engine

Plastic disc brake covers

Touring Motorcycles

MOTORCYCLE TOURING MEANS experiencing the landscape that you travel through at first hand – rather than observing from the enclosed isolation of a car. Riders take off for a weekend trip or a round-the-world adventure – a touring motorcycle can be any machine from a moped to a megabike. Riders favour different approaches to motorcycle touring: some travel with only a credit card and a toothbrush; others take everything from folding chairs to hot water bottles. Transporting everything necessary for two people on a five-week camping tour requires ingenuity and common sense, if handling problems are to be avoided.

A trailer can vastly increase the carrying capacity of any motorcycle. A flexible coupling allows the bike to be leant into corners as normal.

SPECIFICATIONS

1971 BMW R75/5
- **ENGINE** Transverse, horizontally opposed, two cylinder
- **CAPACITY** 745cc
- **POWER OUTPUT** 50bhp @ 6,200rpm
- **TRANSMISSION** Four-speed gearbox, shaft drive
- **FRAME** Duplex cradle
- **SUSPENSION** Telescopic forks, rear twin-shock swingarm
- **WEIGHT** 210kg (463lb)
- **TOP SPEED** 175km/h (109mph)

The back rack is ideal for carrying lightweight luggage

1971 BMW R75/5
The rugged simplicity of BMW machines make them a favourite choice for touring riders. Their combination of reliability and comfort is ideal for covering long distances, and BMW are one of the few companies to take the needs of touring riders seriously.

Map pocket with clear plastic window

A tank bag creates invaluable storage space for maps and valuables, and also takes the wind off the rider's chest

The rack is bolted to the frame

Panniers are fitted to either side of the rear wheel. Some riders prefer the less expensive PVC or canvas versions

Low-maintenance shaft final-drive unit

Reliable, flexible engine allows comfortable cruising rather than high speed

Touring riders value tyre longevity

1982 Honda Gold Wing GL1100 with sidecar and trailer
In motorcycle touring, two schools of thought exist: those who travel with only the bare essentials, and those who take all the comforts of home with them. Honda Gold Wings are popular with the latter category; many owners equip the bikes with accessories to allow them to carry even more luggage, and to make them more comfortable or more individual.

SPECIFICATIONS

1982 Honda GL1100

- ENGINE Four-stroke, water-cooled, flat four
- CAPACITY 1085cc
- POWER OUTPUT 90bhp @ 7,500rpm
- TRANSMISSION Five-speed gearbox, shaft drive
- FRAME Tubular cradle
- SUSPENSION Telescopic forks, rear swingarm, independently sprung sidecar
- WEIGHT 307kg (677lb) (bike only)
- TOP SPEED 185km/h (115mph) (bike only)

Lightweight, glass-fibre Shoreline trailer, with additional racks

Rear top-box also has a rack for extra baggage

Back rest

Citizens' Band radio aerial

A good headlight is a fundamental requirement for long-distance night riding

The California sidecar carries its own lights and indicators

The bike and the sidecar have tinted windscreens

Highway footrests

Disc-brake cover

DID YOU KNOW?

In 1912, Carl Stevens Clancy was the first motorcyclist to travel around-the-world: approximately 18,000 miles (29,000km) from the USA, through Europe, Africa, Japan, and back to New York.

The Elephant Rally
Rallies are a focus for touring motorcyclists. The most famous of these is the Elephant Rally which is held in Germany in the depths of winter (right). Riders from all over Europe travel huge distances, generally in freezing conditions, to attend and camp at the rally (above).

Kawasaki Z1

T HE INDUSTRIAL GIANT, Kawasaki, produces aircraft, robots, bridges, and boats; motorcycles make up only a small part of the company's total output. Production began in the late 1940s, but output never matched that of their main competitors. Their serious challenge in the world market began in the 1960s. In 1969, the remarkable three-cylinder two-stroke won a World Championship and established Kawasaki as makers of high-performance machines. Their reputation soared with the introduction of the Z1 in 1973: Kawasaki's first four-stroke out-performed Honda's 750, and acquired an excellent record for reliability.

Oval rear light

Short rear mudguard

The rear view of the Z1 is a visual feast of glittering symmetry.

1973 Kawasaki Z1
The Z1's performance, good looks, and low price made it the superbike of the mid-seventies. Its success continued unchallenged until Suzuki paid Kawasaki the compliment of copying the engine design in their own big four-stroke. Twenty years later, eight-valve Kawasaki engines based on the Z1 design are still in production.

The co-ordinated tank and tailpiece contributed to the Z1's fine styling

900
DOUBLE OVERHEAD CAMSHAFT

The handsome four-pipe exhaust was expensive to make, and was discontinued

In addition to electric starters, kickstarters continued to be fitted until the late seventies

Brake

900
DOUBLE OVERHEAD CAMSHAFT

There had never been a production machine as powerful as the Z1. The best that Kawasaki's closest competitor, Honda, could boast was a 750cc with a single camshaft.

The famous French endurance race team of Godier/Genoud (Genoud is seen above racing at Thruxton in 1975) were among those riders who competed very successfully using the four-cylinder Kawasaki Z1.

Brake master cylinder

The high, wide handlebars were impractical for a high performance motorcycle

The indicators are housed in chrome mounts

Early frames had a tendency to flex around the head-stock. Bracing was added, but the handling was never ideal

The single front disc brake did not supply adequate stopping power for a machine as powerful as the Z1

Side reflectors are compulsory in America

The 903cc engine is the heart of the Z1, and derivatives are still produced

SPECIFICATIONS

Kawasaki Z1

- **ENGINE** Double-overhead-camshaft, in-line four-cylinder
- **BORE AND STROKE** 66 x 66mm (2⅗ x 2⅗in)
- **CAPACITY** 903cc
- **POWER OUTPUT** 82bhp @ 8,500rpm
- **CARBURATION** Four Mikuni VM28
- **IGNITION** Twelve-volt battery and coil
- **TRANSMISSION** Five-speed gearbox, chain drive
- **CLUTCH** Wet multiplate
- **FRAME** Tubular cradle
- **SUSPENSION** Telescopic forks, rear swingarm
- **BRAKES** Single disc front, drum rear brake
- **WEIGHT** 229.5kg (506lb)
- **TOP SPEED** 211km/h (131mph)
- **YEAR OF CONSTRUCTION** 1973

Kawasaki

UNLIKE MOST JAPANESE companies, Kawasaki were never keen to pursue the market for small-capacity commuter machines. Instead Kawasaki nurtured a reputation as builders of performance machines for enthusiasts, and have remained the smallest of the four big Japanese manufacturers.

Early Kawasaki motorcycles used the logo designed for the firm's heavy industries.

1965 Kawasaki W1

Japanese design progressed and adapted rapidly. The W1 is a superficial copy of the BSA Star Twin (p.69) and was the largest motorcycle produced in Japan in the early sixties. However, design soon moved on.

British-style engine and gearbox construction

The hydraulic steering damper prevents erratic handling

Rear shock absorbers with chrome shrouds

Oil tank for dry sump lubrication

Right foot gearchange

Twin leading-shoe drum brake

SPECIFICATIONS

1965 Kawasaki W1
- **ENGINE** Overhead-valve twin
- **CAPACITY** 624cc
- **POWER OUTPUT** 53bhp @ 7,000rpm
- **TRANSMISSION** Four-speed gearbox, chain drive
- **FRAME** Tubular cradle
- **SUSPENSION** Telescopic forks, rear swingarm
- **WEIGHT** 216kg (476lb)
- **TOP SPEED** 174km/h (108mph)

The three-pipe exhaust layout is unique to the Kawasaki triple.

1970 H1 Mach III

The Kawasaki triple was launched in 1969 and soon gained a reputation for awesome performance and marginal handling. Few road bikes, whatever their capacity, could compete with its reputation for speed and acceleration.

MACH III 500

Tank badge

Air filter

Friction damper

Twin leading-shoe drum brake

Oil-pump cover

Oil-level sight-glass

SPECIFICATIONS

1970 Kawasaki H1 Mach III
- **ENGINE** Two-stroke triple
- **CAPACITY** 498cc
- **POWER OUTPUT** 60bhp @ 8,000rpm
- **TRANSMISSION** Five-speed gearbox, chain drive
- **FRAME** Tubular steel cradle
- **SUSPENSION** Telescopic forks, rear swingarm
- **WEIGHT** 180kg (400lb) (estimated)
- **TOP SPEED** 192km/h (119mph)

Kork Ballington won the 250 and 350cc world titles in 1978 and 1979 on disc-valve twins.

Stripped of its fairing the KR250's innovative engine layout is clearly seen.

Green is the traditional Kawasaki racing colour

The seat unit profile is designed for least drag.

SPECIFICATIONS

1979 Kawasaki KR250

- **ENGINE** Water-cooled rotary-valve twin-cylinder two stroke
- **CAPACITY** 249cc
- **POWER OUTPUT** 68bhp
- **TRANSMISSION** Six-speed gearbox, chain drive
- **FRAME** Tubular steel cradle
- **SUSPENSION** Telescopic forks, rear monoshock Kayaba suspension unit
- **WEIGHT** 104kg (229lb)
- **TOP SPEED** 241km/h (150mph)

1979 Kawasaki KR250

Disc-valve two strokes had proved their potential superiority but the penalty was excessive engine width. By mounting two cylinders one behind the other and using two crankshafts, Kawasaki made the KR250 the same width as a single cylinder bike. This example won the 250cc title in 1979, the second of four consecutive wins for the KR250. A 350cc version was also very successful.

Brake master cylinder

Advanced suspension design used a single damper with an alloy swingarm

Cast alloy wheels

Drilled disc

The rear cylinder's exhaust exits at high level

1984 Kawasaki Z1300

In the late seventies and early eighties Japanese designers continued to increase power and weight. Unfortunately they did this without attending to the problem of the marginal handling characteristics of the machines. The Z1300 is the supreme example of the "bigger is better" philosophy.

Shaft-drive casing

Fuel injector

Bikini fairing with square headlight

Oil cooler

Radiator

SPECIFICATIONS

1984 Kawasaki Z1300

- **ENGINE** Double overhead-camshaft water-cooled in-line six cylinder
- **CAPACITY** 1286cc
- **POWER OUTPUT** 120bhp @ 8,000rpm
- **TRANSMISSION** Five-speed gearbox, shaft drive
- **FRAME** Tubular cradle
- **SUSPENSION** Telescopic forks, rear swingarm
- **WEIGHT** 296kg (653lb)
- **TOP SPEED** 217km/h (135mph)

Suzuki RT63

BEFORE THE SECOND WORLD WAR, Suzuki built weaving equipment. The decline of the Japanese weaving industry drove them to research a new product, and join the post-war rush to produce cheap vehicles. Their first prototype motorbike was built in 1951 and was no more than a very crude motorized bicycle; production began the next year. In 1955 Suzuki built their first true motorcycle, a simple 125cc two-stroke with three gears. They developed rapidly, initially building two-strokes but moving into four-strokes in the seventies. In 1961 they followed Honda's lead and began exporting. They also followed Honda into Grand Prix racing, entering their first TT in 1960. Their first World Championship was the 50cc class in 1962.

New Zealander, Hugh Anderson, won four World Championships for Suzuki. He won the 1963 125cc Championship on the bike below.

1963 Suzuki GP RT63
MZ rider, Ernst Degner, joined Suzuki at the end of 1961, bringing with him the secrets of advanced two-stroke design; even so, the 1962 125 Suzuki single was beaten by the four-stroke Hondas. For 1963, Suzuki built an all-new twin. The RT63 was competitive for one season only. In 1964, the four-cylinder Hondas were dominant, and in the 125cc Championship Suzuki rider Hugh Anderson could only finish third.

Suede seat cover

Heat shield

Twin leading-shoe rear brake

Narrow-section racing tyres minimize friction

The cassette-type gearbox can be removed without dismantling the crankcases, allowing gear ratios to be changed easily

Early Japanese racing two-strokes had very narrow power bands, and were prone to seizing. Water-cooling helped to prevent this. Carburettor settings had a critical effect on mixture strength and reliability.

Dry clutch

Solo racing seat and tailpiece

The remote float-bowl is flexibly mounted to prevent the fuel from frothing

Chest pad supports prone rider

Rev counter

Fairing mounting

Cable splitter

Frame bracing

Disc valves are concealed behind alloy covers. The fuel mixture enters directly to the crankcase

Rear-facing exhaust ports were used despite problems dissipating heat from an air-cooled motor

The front brake is twin-sided

— DID YOU KNOW? —
The usable power generated by this kind of two-stroke racer was sometimes within a very small range of engine revs: just 500rpm.

SPECIFICATIONS

Suzuki RT63

- **ENGINE** Disc-valve two-stroke twin
- **BORE AND STROKE** 43 x 42.6mm (1⅜ x 1¼in)
- **CAPACITY** 124cc
- **POWER OUTPUT** 25.5bhp @ 12,000rpm
- **CARBURATION** Two Mikuni carburettors with remote float bowls
- **IGNITION** Magneto
- **TRANSMISSION** Eight-speed gearbox, chain drive
- **CLUTCH** Dry multiplate
- **FRAME** Tubular cradle
- **SUSPENSION** Telescopic forks, rear swingarm
- **BRAKES** Front double-side drum, twin leading-shoe rear drum
- **WEIGHT** 94kg (207lb)
- **TOP SPEED** 184km/h (114mph)
- **YEAR OF CONSTRUCTION** 1963

Suzuki

SUZUKI WITHDREW FROM RACING to develop motocross and road bikes. They won their first motocross World Championship in 1970, and introduced the first of a new range of two-stroke triples the following year. When a short-lived Wankel-engined model failed to sell, Suzuki began building four-strokes in 1976, using the superb double overhead-camshaft Kawasaki (pp.120-21) as their starting point. In the seventies, Suzuki also made a successful return to Grand Prix racing with a 500cc disc-valve two-stroke.

1968 Suzuki TC250
The TC250 was a trail-style American version of Suzuki's X6 or Super Six model, launched in 1965. The largest Suzuki of its time, combining excellent performance, a six-speed gearbox, and automatic lubrication, the X6 helped to establish Suzuki's reputation worldwide.

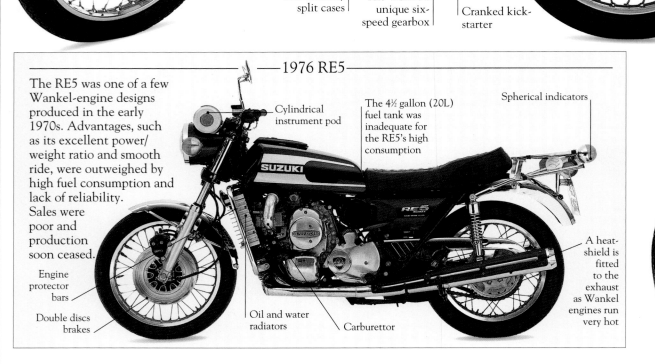

Textured rubber knee pads

Ignition lock

The alloy barrels have iron cylinder liners

Horizontally split cases

The TC250's unique six-speed gearbox

Cranked kick-starter

Anti-dive valves prevent forks plunging when braking

1976 RE5

The RE5 was one of a few Wankel-engine designs produced in the early 1970s. Advantages, such as its excellent power/weight ratio and smooth ride, were outweighed by high fuel consumption and lack of reliability. Sales were poor and production soon ceased.

Cylindrical instrument pod

The 4½ gallon (20L) fuel tank was inadequate for the RE5's high consumption

Spherical indicators

Engine protector bars

Double discs brakes

Oil and water radiators

Carburettor

A heat-shield is fitted to the exhaust as Wankel engines run very hot

SPECIFICATIONS

1971 Suzuki GT750

- **ENGINE** Two-stroke water-cooled triple
- **CAPACITY** 738cc
- **POWER OUTPUT** 67bhp @ 6,500rpm
- **TRANSMISSION** Five-speed gearbox, chain drive
- **FRAME** Duplex cradle
- **SUSPENSION** Telescopic forks, rear swingarm
- **WEIGHT** 238kg (524lb)
- **TOP SPEED** 174km/h (108mph)

1971 Suzuki GT750

Suzuki entered the Superbike market in 1971 with this unusual three-cylinder, water-cooled two-stroke, nicknamed "Water Buffaloes" in America, and "Kettles" in Britain. A successful racing version was also built. Large-capacity two-strokes were effectively killed off in the mid 1970s, by strict emission controls, and Suzuki began building four strokes.

The Suzuki's instruments include a centrally mounted water-temperature gauge.

Radiator fan

Exuberant paintwork and styling became more subdued in later models

Passenger grab-rail

The drum brake, with four leading shoes, gave way to discs on later models

Cylinder water jacket

Three cylinders exit into four exhaust pipes

1982 Suzuki Katana

Suzuki commissioned the Katana styling from Target Design of Germany. The bikes were based on the existing, large-capacity four-cylinder models that were capable but bland. The addition of radical styling transformed them into classics. The Katana was eventually outmoded by a new generation of sports machines.

Katana is the name of the Japanese sword shown in the logo.

SPECIFICATIONS

1982 Suzuki Katana

- **ENGINE** Double overhead-camshaft sixteen-valve four cylinder
- **CAPACITY** 997cc
- **POWER OUTPUT** 108bhp
- **TRANSMISSION** Five-speed gearbox, chain drive
- **FRAME** Tubular cradle
- **SUSPENSION** Telescopic forks, rear swingarm
- **WEIGHT** 251kg (554lb)
- **TOP SPEED** 225km/h (140mph)

Fuel tap

Regulator

Brake discs have cooling slots

The sixteen-valve, four-cylinder engine was developed from an eight-valve

Adjustable shock absorbers

Yamaha

YAMAHA FOLLOWED HONDA into the world market and international racing, producing highly effective two-stroke machines that set high standards of performance and reliability. From 1961 to 1968 they won several world championships and led suspension technology during the 1970s with cantilever rear suspension systems. Four-stroke development resulted in significant technical advances such as the first five-valve cylinder heads and variable exhaust valve control.

SPECIFICATIONS

1965 Yamaha YDS3C Big Bear
- **ENGINE** Two-stroke twin
- **CAPACITY** 246cc
- **POWER OUTPUT** 21bhp @ 7,500rpm
- **TRANSMISSION** Five-speed gearbox, chain drive
- **FRAME** Twin-tube cradle
- **SUSPENSION** Telescopic forks, rear swingarm
- **WEIGHT** 159kg (350lb)
- **TOP SPEED** 142km/h (88mph)

1965 Yamaha YDS3C Big Bear

Two-stroke twins such as the Big Bear established Yamaha's excellent reputation for good performance. High-level exhaust pipes, originally designed for off-road use, are fitted to what is essentially a road bike.

A hand pump, mounted under the tank, formed part of the tool kit

Automatic lubrication system

Heat shield

Combined speedometer and rev counter

Fork springs are mounted outside of the damper units

Yamaha's two-stroke twin cylinder engine is one of the longest lasting designs in motorcycle history

High level exhaust pipes were fashionable in America

1974 Yamaha YZ250

Yamaha won the 250cc Motocross World Championship in 1973. In the following year they introduced the monoshock suspension system that has since become commonplace on both road and competition machinery. The YZ250 became enormously popular with amateur motocross riders.

A spark arrestor prevents sparks escaping from the exhaust

The bodywork of the YZ250 is easily removed for maintenance.

Shock absorber gas reservoir

Racing number plate

SPECIFICATIONS

1974 Yamaha YZ250
- **ENGINE** Air-cooled two-stroke single cylinder
- **CAPACITY** 246cc
- **POWER OUTPUT** 21bhp @ 7,500rpm
- **TRANSMISSION** Five-speed gearbox, chain drive
- **FRAME** Tubular cradle
- **SUSPENSION** Telescopic forks and rear cantilever
- **WEIGHT** 159kg (350lb)
- **TOP SPEED** 141.5km/h (88mph)

Powerful air-cooled single cylinder engine

Air filter

The Exup, complete with its full fairing, is shown left. Below, the dohc four-cylinder engine is exposed for inspection.

1992 Yamaha FZR1000 Exup
Yamaha only began building four strokes in the late 1960s, but they caught up fast. The FZ series of five-valve-per-cylinder engines were introduced in 1985. The variable exhaust valve, which offers a wider spread of power than would otherwise be available, did not appear until 1989.

The FZR uses upside-down telescopic forks; the lower section of the fork slides into the upper

Three-spoke wheels

Injection-moulded plastic fairing

Twin spar chassis

Radiator

Rear suspension linkage

Exhaust power valve

Flexible mudguards

Conical brake hub

54cm (21in) front wheel

Single shock absorber

High-level exhaust pipe

Bash plate

SPECIFICATIONS
1992 Yamaha FZR1000 Exup
- **ENGINE** Double overhead-camshaft water-cooled four cylinder
- **CAPACITY** 1002cc
- **POWER OUTPUT** 125bhp @ 10,000rpm
- **TRANSMISSION** Six-speed, chain drive
- **FRAME** Twin spar
- **SUSPENSION** Upside-down telescopic forks, rear swingarm with rising rate single shock
- **WEIGHT** 240kg (529lb)
- **TOP SPEED** 269km/h (167mph)

The Exup's air scoops feed the air box to supply the down-draught carburettors.

Daylight driving light

Air scoops

Horn

---- DID YOU KNOW? ----
The Yamaha logo is composed of three tuning forks, because the company originally manufactured musical instruments. Torakusu Yamaha built the first Yamaha organ in 1887, and the company has since become one the world's largest musical instrument manufacturers. The Yamaha Motor Company was founded in 1955.

Yamaha TR3

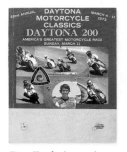

Y AMAHA REGARDED RACING as a marketing exercise and a testing ground for new technology. Their first efforts on the international circuits were not a great success, but their commitment was rewarded: they won the 250cc World Championship in 1964 and 1965, the 125cc title in 1967, and both championships in 1968. Yamaha then withdrew their factory machines from the championship and for a long period only supplied production racers to private race teams. These racers were heavily based on the road bikes, but achieved spectacular results. Competition improved the racers and improvements filtered back to road bikes, which in turn gained cantilever suspension and water-cooling.

Don Emde (centre) on 1973 Daytona programme

Don Emde, winner of the 1972 Daytona 200 mile race, with the winner's flag and trophy. Emde's father, Floyd, won the race in 1948.

1972 Yamaha TR3

One of a long series of highly successful Yamaha production racers, the TR3 was the last of their air-cooled machines, just predating the all-conquering water-cooled TZ models. This machine, ridden by Don Emde, won the 1972 Daytona 200 mile race. The TR3 was the smallest-capacity machine ever to win the event and was the first of twelve consecutive Yamaha victories.

The seat hump used at Daytona was larger and more aerodynamic than this short-circuit type

Increased fuel-tank capacity meant fewer pit stops

For safety, a plastic shampoo bottle catches overflow from the gearbox oil breather

The box section swingarm is more rigid than a tubular swing-arm, and allows a wider tyre to be fitted

Crucial components are safety-wired to prevent them from working loose

Expansion chamber exhaust

A dry clutch is a racing component, lighter and stronger than the wet type

Coloured leathers appeared in the late 1960s.

Don Emde's 1972 race leathers

The rider's boot is worn away as a result of rubbing the track at corners

The speed of the Daytona circuit makes aerodynamics crucial. Here Emde crouches out of the wind on the banked section of the course where the highest speeds are achieved. His average speed was 166km/h (103.35mph). Number 99 is Ray Hempstead who finished second.

Yamaha tuning fork logo

YAMAHA

Simple fixings allow the fairing to be removed in seconds for access to the engine

An electronic ignition control box is mounted under the fairing stay

Frame gussets give extra strength

Exhaust retaining springs

Road-bike engines had an oil pump fitted here. Racers used oil mixed with the petrol for lubrication

Four-leading-shoe drum brake with cutaways to allow air cooling

Lead wire is wrapped around the spokes to balance the wheel

SPECIFICATIONS

Yamaha TR3

- **ENGINE** Two-stroke twin
- **BORE AND STROKE** 64 x 54mm (2½ x 2⅛in)
- **CAPACITY** 347cc
- **POWER OUTPUT** 58bhp @ 9,000rpm
- **CARBURATION** Two Mikuni carburettors
- **IGNITION** Magneto
- **TRANSMISSION** Six-speed gearbox, chain drive
- **CLUTCH** Dry multiplate
- **FRAME** Tubular cradle
- **SUSPENSION** Telescopic forks, rear swingarm
- **BRAKES** Double-sided drum brakes, single-sided rear drums
- **WEIGHT** 106.5kg (235lb)
- **TOP SPEED** Not recorded
- **YEAR OF CONSTRUCTION** 1972

The Rest of the World

Motorcycles are built around the globe from the factories of
Brazil to the specialized workshops of Byelorussia.

Motorcycles have been built all over the world from Korea to Canada, Belgium to Brazil. America, Germany, and Britain have all been home to the world's largest motorcycle industries; each country still has a single manufacturer of high-quality, prestige motorcycles. In other countries, such as France, which boasted a significant motorcycle industry, almost nothing remains.

1924 Terrot

The Bultaco logo

Motorcycles and the National Economy

The performance of a nation's motorcycle industry is an indicator of its economic state. Many companies in Belgium and France closed in the fifties and sixties, after a long period of decline. The relative prosperity of their national economies meant that more people could afford to buy cars so that the demand for motorcycles declined. Long-established Belgian companies FN and Sarolea also stopped building motorcycles in the late fifties. In Holland, the Eysink company had to close in 1956, after more than half a century's production. In France only mopeds are still in production. In Spain, motorcycle manufacture only began in the 1940s: simple, cheap, two-strokes were initially intended for the protected domestic market. Off-road machines were exported to much of Europe and America during the sixties and seventies until tariff restrictions were removed, undermining the home industry. Increasingly widespread wealth meant that the population began to buy cars in greater numbers, rather than motorcycles.

1992 Husqvarna Motocross TC610

Nimbus sales literature

Eastern Europe and Asia

The collapse of the Iron Curtain has exposed several Eastern European motorcycle manufacturers to the harsh realities of the market economy. Czechoslovakia had a very healthy industry before the Second World War. The firm of Laurin and Klement were amongst the first European manufacturers, and many other Czechoslovakian companies followed their lead. Under Communist control only two significant makes, Jawa and CZ, existed. Both were produced in large numbers for home and export markets; however, their future development is difficult to predict. As established industries have shrunk or closed down, new ones have sprung up. Machines made in India, Korea, China, and Taiwan are beginning to appear in world export markets. Japanese manufacturers have since established factories in many countries, far from Japan: in the last decade motorcycles carrying the names of Yamaha and Honda have been built as far away as Brazil.

North and South

Motorcycles are built all over the world. As early as 1913, an advanced four-valve single-cylinder bike was built in Australia. It was called a Rova-Kent; production only lasted from 1913 until 1914. Tilbrook was launched in 1950 but closed down again in 1953. In Canada, snowmobile makers Bombardier, produced many competition machines under the name Can-Am during the seventies and eighties. A huge machine called an Amazonas, using a Volkswagen Beetle car engine, was built in Brazil. Limited numbers of Britten racing machines are produced in New Zealand. New makes are launched and familiar ones disappear, contributing to the evolution of the motorcycle.

1927 Böhmerland

Austria

AUSTRIA'S FIRST production motorcycles were built by Püch in 1903. Other Austrian manufacturers followed, but none of them were as successful or established a comparable international reputation, until the emergence of the KTM company in the 1960s. Püch are still in business, although they now only make mopeds.

SPECIFICATIONS
1926 Püch 220
- **ENGINE** Split single two-stroke
- **CAPACITY** 223cc
- **POWER OUTPUT** 4.5bhp
- **TRANSMISSION** No gearbox, chain drive
- **FRAME** Tubular cradle
- **SUSPENSION** Girder forks, no rear suspension
- **WEIGHT** 77kg (170lb)
- **TOP SPEED** 72.5km/h (45mph)

1926 Püch 220
The two-stroke split single was first developed by Adalberto Garelli in 1912. Püch adopted and developed the idea from 1923 and continued with the design for nearly half a century.

Oil and petrol are stored in separate compartments within the tank

Parking brake lever

Clutch in rear hub, no gearbox

Chain connects engine directly to rear wheel

Kickstart lever

Rear brake pedal

Drum brake

KTM

KTM was founded in 1953 and began by building a variety of small-capacity two-stroke mopeds, scooters, and motorcycles, using Rotax engines. The success of KTM's competition bikes, using their own design of engines, established an international reputation.

1979 KTM 246cc
Russian rider, Gennady Moisseyev, won the 250cc Motocross Championship riding a KTM in 1974. By this time, nearly all competition bikes were using engines designed and built by KTM themselves (as seen on the bike below), rather than using engines manufactured by Rotax.

High-level exhaust pipe

Angled shock absorbers

Flexible mudguards

Lightweight magnesium alloy fork sliders

Front springs are extended rather than compressed

Unusual colour scheme

Czechoslovakia

CZECHOSLOVAKIA'S first motorcycles were built in 1899 by Laurin and Klement. Before the Second World War a healthy industry existed; after the war, Jawa and CZ survived as nationalized industries working closely together. Jawa were famous for their speedway bikes while CZ won several Motocross World Championships.

Braced handlebars

Radially finned cylinder head

Quick-action throttle

Dirt shield

Light, strong construction is typical of a speedway machine.

1974 CZ Motocrosser
CZ were nationalized after the war but continued to build their two-stroke machines as well as ohc road racers. During the 1960s they produced excellent motocross bikes that won world championships several times.

1966 Eso Speedway
Eso first built speedway bikes in 1949. Jawa took over Eso in 1962 and still build speedway bikes, although Eso's name was dropped.

Air filter

Oil tank (Engine lubrication is constant loss)

The valve emerges from the side of the tyre in case the cover creeps around the wheel rim

SPECIFICATIONS
1974 CZ Motocrosser
- **ENGINE** Two-stroke single
- **CAPACITY** 380cc
- **POWER OUTPUT** 42bhp @ 6,800rpm
- **TRANSMISSION** Four-speed gearbox, chain drive
- **FRAME** Tubular steel cradle
- **SUSPENSION** Telescopic forks, rear swingarm with twin shocks
- **WEIGHT** Not known
- **TOP SPEED** 121km/h (75mph)

SPECIFICATIONS
1966 Eso Speedway
- **ENGINE** Four-stroke air-cooled single
- **CAPACITY** 497cc
- **POWER OUTPUT** 50bhp @ 8,000rpm
- **TRANSMISSION** Single speed, chain drive
- **FRAME** Tubular open cradle with stressed engine
- **SUSPENSION** Telescopic forks, no rear suspension
- **WEIGHT** 83kg (182lb)
- **TOP SPEED** Dependent on gearing

1927 Böhmerland
These extraordinary machines were built from 1925 until 1939. They were designed by Albin Liebisch, who also designed the engine which bears his name. A more conventional-looking, short wheelbase model was also built, and even used in competition. Production was halted by the advent of the Second World War.

Tool box

Exposed valve gear

Seating for three people

Fuel tanks are positioned either side of the rear wheel

Early example of one-piece cast alloy wheels

SPECIFICATIONS
1927 Böhmerland
- **ENGINE** Overhead-valve single
- **CAPACITY** 603cc
- **POWER OUTPUT** 16hp @ 3,000rpm
- **TRANSMISSION** Three-speed gearbox, chain drive
- **FRAME** Welded tube
- **SUSPENSION** Leading link forks, no rear suspension
- **WEIGHT** 227kg (500lb)
- **TOP SPEED** 95km/h (59mph)

France

T HE DESIGN OF THE internal combustion engine, first developed in Germany, was advanced by the French partnership of De Dion and Bouton: also selling engines, they helped to found a thriving industry in France at the end of the last century. France became a centre for motor sport; the first motorcycle race was the Paris-Nantes of 1896, and the first official international closed-road race was the Cup of 1904, followed by the first Grand Prix (pp.144-7) in 1913. France built motorbikes until mopeds and cheaper cars, such as the Citröen 2CV, ended its popularity as a means of transport.

Established in 1899, Peugeot went on to build advanced overhead-camshaft racing machines (as seen above).

1907 Deronzière

Deronzière produced motorcycles from 1903 until the outbreak of the First World War. They built their own 282cc engines, and also used motors supplied by Peugeot, and the Swiss firm Zedel. Deronzières were well-designed, compact bikes which remained popular throughout their short production run.

SPECIFICATIONS

1907 Deronzière
- ENGINE Inlet-over-exhaust, air-cooled four-stroke single
- CAPACITY 282cc
- POWER OUTPUT 3-5hp (estimated)
- TRANSMISSION Single-speed, belt drive
- FRAME Tubular loop
- SUSPENSION Leading-link forks, no rear suspension
- WEIGHT 49kg (108lb) (estimated)
- TOP SPEED 32km/h (20mph)

Controls to throttle, brakes, and valve lifter

Fuel and oil filler caps

Carburettor

Simple front suspension system

Silencer

Belt tensioner

The pulley is fixed to the rear wheel rim by very short spokes

— RENÉ GILLET —

Established in 1898, René Gillet produced machines noted for their strength and reliability, rather than their sporting ability. They were ideal machines for pulling a sidecar.

René Gillet's most famous bikes were the powerful 750 and 1000cc V-twins which they supplied to the French Police and Army in large numbers. The company diversified to produce a variety of other models and, after the Second World War, chose to concentrate on small-capacity two-strokes. The company remained in business until 1957.

— DID YOU KNOW? —

The 250cc class of the first Grand Prix, held in France in 1913, was won by a rider called Bange, riding a Terrot. The last time a French machine won a Grand Prix, was in the British 250cc in 1983, when Jaques Bolle won on a Pernod.

In 1923 Terrot built a conventional 350cc machine, using a British JAP engine and a variable-belt drive system. They soon developed their own engine for the machine, gradually evolving it over the following years. The 500cc overhead-valve machine was the company's most famous product. This model features a huge chromed headlamp. Many successful 500cc production racers were also built by Terrot.

The first Terrots were built in Dijon in 1902. In the late twenties they moved to a large new factory that was among the most modern in Europe. They became part of the Peugeot group in the fifties, but production ceased in the sixties.

Fifties' sales brochures for smaller-capacity Terrot models.

The 500cc Terrots such as the model above, were very common in France, with their distinctive logo, chrome-plated fuel tank, and headlamp. The success of this simple but effective design, is reflected in their popularity with today's restorers and collectors.

1924 Terrot

Charles Terrot's company built a wide variety of machines. In addition to successful racers, they also manufactured simple working motorbikes. The 173cc two stroke, shown below, was a popular and well-made machine. Terrot's motorcycles retained the use of belt final drive long after most manufacturers had abandoned them in favour of chains. Early models used a variable pulley system rather than a gearbox.

Acetylene-powered headlight

SPECIFICATIONS
1924 Terrot
• ENGINE Air-cooled two-stroke single
• CAPACITY 173cc
• POWER OUTPUT 3hp
• TRANSMISSION Two-speed gearbox, belt drive
• FRAME Rigid
• SUSPENSION Parallel slider forks, no rear suspension
• WEIGHT 110kg (242½lb)
• TOP SPEED 60km/h (37mph)

Picnic basket

The gear lever is pushed forward to select a lower gear

The fork legs pivot to provide front suspension

Bicycle-type hand pump

Rim brake

Inclined cylinder with horizontal cooling fins

Spare spark-plug

Scandinavia

THERE HAS NEVER BEEN a large market for motorcycles in Scandinavia, and therefore the industry is relatively small. The Swedish company, Husqvarna, was the biggest, longest-surviving manufacturer, and their competition success has encouraged smaller specialist firms to develop. Lito produced limited numbers of excellent motocross machines in the 1960s, and Husaberg still do today. The celebrated name of Husqvarna lives on, although the machines themselves are now built in Italy.

SPECIFICATIONS

1953 Nimbus 750
- ENGINE In-line, overhead-camshaft, four cylinder
- CAPACITY 746cc
- POWER OUTPUT 22bhp
- TRANSMISSION Three-speed gearbox, shaft drive
- FRAME Pressed steel cradle
- SUSPENSION Telescopic forks, no rear suspension
- WEIGHT 185kg (408lb)
- TOP SPEED 113kmh (70mph)

1935 Nimbus 750

The Danish firm, Nimbus, began making motorcycles in 1919. Production was temporarily halted in 1928, but started again in 1934; at this time the machine underwent a significant redesign. The last of their motorcycles were made in 1959. This model is a military version – the Danish armed forces took a large proportion of Nimbus' production.

A civilian version of the Nimbus is pictured in a post-war brochure.

Pressed steel handlebars

Rubber seat-spring

Tool box

Exposed valve springs

The propstand is mounted on upper frame rail

1935 Husqvarna 500

Husqvarna were armaments manufacturers who diversified their output in 1903 in order to begin motorcycle production. Singles and V-twins were produced using engines that were bought in from other makers. The marque was not well known outside Scandinavia until the introduction of its innovative 350cc and 500cc racers in 1930. At this time, the majority of competition motorcycles in Europe were single-cylinder machines and a V-twin was a novelty. The V-twin was improved but its potential was never fully realized, although these bikes won races in Europe. The factory team withdrew from racing in 1935, but private owners continued to compete using Husqvarnas.

SPECIFICATIONS

1935 Husqvarna 500
- ENGINE Overhead-valve V-twin
- CAPACITY 497cc
- POWER OUTPUT 44bhp @ 6,800rpm
- TRANSMISSION Four-speed gearbox, chain drive
- FRAME Single loop tubular
- SUSPENSION Girder forks, no rear suspension
- WEIGHT 127kg (280lb)
- TOP SPEED 190km/h (118mph)

Conical hub with integral brake drum and sprocket

The Husqvarna rider, Stanley Woods, prior to the start of the 1934 senior TT (right). Woods ran out of petrol while holding second position on the last lap.

1973 Husqvarna Enduro 504WR

Post-war production at Husqvarna centred on two-strokes. Their motocross and enduro bikes were exceptional and, in 1961, production of road bikes ceased. In 1986 Husqvarna sold their manufacturing rights to Cagiva of Italy.

Alloy handlebars

The minimal headlights comply with enduro regulations

Alloy fuel tank

Pressed steel brake lever

Air cleaner and carburettor shroud

Lightweight conical brake hubs

SPECIFICATIONS

1973 Husqvarna 504WR
- **ENGINE** Air-cooled two-stroke single
- **POWER OUTPUT** 32bhp (estimated)
- **CAPACITY** 454cc
- **TRANSMISSION** Five-speed gearbox, chain drive
- **FRAME** Tubular steel cradle
- **SUSPENSION** Telescopic forks and twin-shock rear swingarm
- **WEIGHT** 118kg (260lb) (estimated)
- **TOP SPEED** 153km/h (95mph)

Ploughing a straight furrow, a Husqvarna enduro team rider shows that the bike handles very well even in deep mud.

Carburettor float bowl

Hairpin valve spring

Central spring for girder forks

Wheel balance weights

Chain driven magneto

Oil tank

Gear pedal

Pushrod tubes

Spain

MOTORCYCLE PRODUCTION began in Spain in the 1940s, and thrived for the next three decades. Montesa, Bultaco, and Ossa exported large numbers of off-road machines, and Derbi, who concentrated on manufacturing mopeds, achieved outstanding race success. Industrial unrest in the 1980s depressed the industry. Only Montesa and Derbi survived.

The "thumbs up" Bultaco logo

SPECIFICATIONS

1975 Bultaco Metralla
- **ENGINE** Air-cooled two-stroke single
- **CAPACITY** 244cc
- **POWER OUTPUT** 25bhp
- **TRANSMISSION** Six-speed, chain drive
- **FRAME** Tubular cradle
- **SUSPENSION** Telescopic forks, twin-shock rear swingarm
- **WEIGHT** 123kg (271lb)
- **TOP SPEED** 137 km/h (85mph)

1975 Bultaco Metralla
The Metralla is a typical Spanish road bike, using a single-cylinder two-stroke engine in a conventional chassis. Ossa and Montesa also produced similar bikes. However, in comparison to their international competitors these bikes were crude, and few were ever exported.

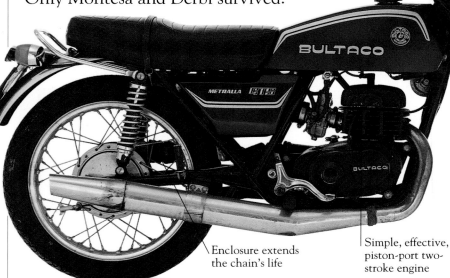

Enclosure extends the chain's life

Simple, effective, piston-port two-stroke engine

Twin leading-shoe front drum brake

Martin Lampkin (right) just before he won the 1975 World Trials title on the bike below.

OSSA

Ossa's World Championship career relied on their highly advanced 250cc single. Santiago Herrero (left), won several Grand Prix on this machine in 1969 and 1970. He was killed in the 1970 TT and the team stopped racing.

Ossa's four-leafed-clover mascot

A prototype 1000cc Ossa: this two-stroke four, which was built in 1972, came to a spectacular end during its first and last race outing (left).

SPECIFICATIONS

1974 Bultaco Sherpa
- **ENGINE** Air-cooled two-stroke single
- **CAPACITY** 348cc
- **POWER OUTPUT** 20bhp
- **TRANSMISSION** Five-speed, chain drive
- **FRAME** Tubular cradle
- **SUSPENSION** Telescopic forks, twin-shock rear swingarm
- **WEIGHT** 100kg (220lb)
- **TOP SPEED** Dependent on gearing
- Figures are for the World Championship-winning version, shown right.

1974 Bultaco Sherpa
The Sherpa was developed by British trials rider Sammy Miller (p.156), in the 1960s, and later became the most successful of the Spanish trials machines. Bultaco then went on to dominate the sport in the 1970s and won the World Trials Championship for five consecutive years from its inauguration in 1975 onwards.

SPECIFICATIONS

1992 Montesa Cota

- **ENGINE** Water-cooled two-stroke single
- **CAPACITY** 258cc
- **POWER OUTPUT** Not measured
- **TRANSMISSION** Six speed, chain drive
- **FRAME** Alloy box-section
- **SUSPENSION** Telescopic forks, single-shock rear swingarm
- **WEIGHT** 83kg (183lb)
- **TOP SPEED** Dependent on gearing

Handlebar bracing aids rigidity

Alloy frame

Snail-cam chain adjuster

Upside-down forks

Bash plate protects the engine

Disc brakes are fitted to front and rear wheels

Drive-chain tensioner

Special alloy rims allow the use of tubeless tyres

1992 Montesa Cota

Montesa was founded in 1944 by Pedro Permanyer and Francisco Bulto; Bulto later left to form his own Bultaco company. They exported off-road bikes in the 1960s and 1970s and won the World Trials championship in 1980. Montesa were among the Spanish firms that suffered difficulties in the eighties, surviving partly through their links with Honda (pp.112-5).

The legendary Impala, Montesa's most successful road bike, ridden by European Cup winner Carlos Rocamora.

Chromed-alloy handlebars are wide for greater control

Steering has an excellent lock range

Extremely narrow fuel tank

High-level exhaust

Enlarged-capacity works engine

53cm (21in) front wheel

Lightweight front drum-brake

PORTUGAL

Casal are the only motorcycle manufacturer presently operating in Portugal. Originally founded in 1966, they started by producing machines using Zündapp engines. They soon developed their own two-stroke power units. Although Casal have built some machines larger than 50cc, the bulk of their production is devoted to this size of machine (see bottom left). The engine is a conventional piston-port two-stroke; sports models also have water cooling. Very few have been exported. Some trials and motocross machines (see top left) were also designed and built by Casal.

Motorcycle Sport

MOTORCYCLE SPORT began when two motorcyclists first met. True enthusiasts have always wanted to know which is the fastest, most reliable machine, and makers have always wanted to gain prestige for their bikes. Motorcycles are raced all over the world, from the Sahara Desert to the frozen lakes of Russia: on sand, ice, mud, and custom-built tracks.

Grand Prix Racing

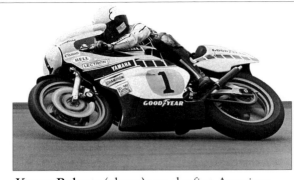

THE FRENCH GRAND PRIX was first run in 1913, but the name "Grand Prix" was later given to any prestigious international race. The World Championships, made up of a series of Grand Prix races, were organized in 1949, although the 1961 Argentine Grand Prix was the first championship race held outside Europe. Early British successes were surpassed by Italian machines. In the 1970s, Japanese two-strokes dominated the premier 500cc class.

Kenny Roberts (above) was the first American rider to win a World Championship. He won the 500cc class for Yamaha at his first attempt in 1978, then won again in 1979 and 1980.

Rev counter

Carburettors

One exhaust pipe exits over the engine to provide ground clearance

Slick rear tyre

The four expansion-chamber exhausts are given adequate ground clearance by contorting the exhaust pipes. The pipe exiting by the seat comes from the cylinder on the far left.

1979 Yamaha OW48

Yamaha's piston-ported two-strokes were the most widely used and successful racing machines of the 1970s, in every class from 125 to 750cc. Giacomo Agostini won Yamaha's first 500cc world title in 1975, then Barry Sheene won in 1976 and 1977 on the superior disc-valve Suzuki. The riding skills of Kenny Roberts negated the Suzuki advantage, and he won the world title for Yamaha in 1978, 1979 (on the bike seen here), and 1980.

Clip-on bars

Ignition coils

Yellow and black were Yamaha's American racing colours in the late 1970s

Radiator cap

Power Valve

Morris seven-spoke alloy wheels

Damping adjustment screws

SPECIFICATIONS

Yamaha OW48

- **ENGINE** In-line two-stroke four cylinder
- **BORE AND STROKE** 56 x 50.5mm
- **CAPACITY** 498cc
- **POWER OUTPUT** 130bhp
- **CARBURATION** 4 x Mikuni
- **IGNITION** Electronic
- **TRANSMISSION** Six-speed gearbox, chain drive
- **CLUTCH** Dry multiplate
- **FRAME** Tubular steel cradle
- **SUSPENSION** Telescopic forks, rear mono shock
- **BRAKES** Twin disc brakes front, single disc rear
- **WEIGHT** 145kg (320lb)
- **TOP SPEED** 290 km/h (180 mph)
- **YEAR OF CONSTRUCTION** 1979

Riders wait for the flag to drop at the start of the 1979 British Grand Prix. Eventual winner, Kenny Roberts is pictured second from left, push-starting the Yamaha. Barry Sheene, who finished second, is seen furthest in line from the camera.

RIDING STYLES

The 500cc class has always been considered the premier Grand Prix class, but there are also world championship classes for 125 and 250cc solos. Classes for 50, 80 and 350cc machines also used to be contested. Racing in the smaller classes (as in the 1992 Spanish 125cc GP, top left) is often closer than in 500cc races. Top riders are separated by fractions of a second at the end of a race, and the lead can change many times in one lap.

Racers used to compete in several GP classes during the same race season but the increased sophistication of today's bikes makes it difficult for riders to change capacity classes. In the smaller classes riders concentrate on achieving a high cornering speed. 500cc riders exploit the extra power of their machines and adopt a more aggressive style. Successful 250cc rider Luca Cadalora (bottom left) takes a corner in the smooth style typical of a 250cc race.

Tubular box-section steel frame

The seat design is spartan, as comfort is not a priority

The nuts holding critical components in place are "lock-wired" into position for safety

Cooling duct

Gearchange linkage

Alloy swingarm

Grand Prix Racing

GRAND PRIX RACING has changed radically over the years. The circuits have become safer; perilous road circuits, such as the one on the Isle of Man, are no longer included in the bike championship. As a result of the ever-escalating cost of racing, bikes carry more and more advertising. The popularity of the sport has grown, and television coverage has increased. In the constant search for more power and speed, new machines have to evolve very quickly: a motorcycle that is competitive for one season may well be hopelessly outclassed in the next. As well as being a good opportunity to promote the manufacturer's name, racing is a vital stimulus for the development of new designs. Improvements made to Grand Prix racers do eventually find their way onto production machines.

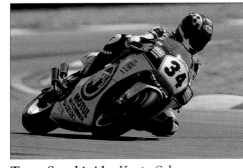

Team-Suzuki rider Kevin Schwantz (shown in action above), won the 500cc category in the Italian Grand Prix in 1992.

1992 Suzuki RGV500
In the competitive world of Grand Prix racing, manufacturers strive to give their products the edge over the opposition. With 170 bhp available on modern Grand Prix machines, lack of power is not a problem. Most modifications are intended to harness this level of energy and make the bikes easier to control.

The seat hump contains computerized data-recording equipment that monitors the bike's performance

The rear cylinder exhausts exit above the rear wheel

The silencers are made from carbon fibre

One-piece seat and tail unit

Rear disc-brake master cylinder

Transferring 170bhp onto the tarmac track requires the correct tyre. Grand Prix races are often won or lost as a result of tyre choice.

The swingarm is arched to provide clearance for exhausts

SPECIFICATIONS

Suzuki RGV500

- **ENGINE** Twin crank V-four water-cooled two-stroke
- **BORE AND STROKE** 56 x 50.6mm (2¼x 2in)
- **CAPACITY** 498cc
- **POWER OUTPUT** 170bhp @ 13,000rpm
- **CARBURATION** Two twin choke flat slide carbs
- **IGNITION** Computer controlled self-generating
- **TRANSMISSION** Six-speed cassette type, chain drive
- **CLUTCH** Dry multiplate
- **FRAME** Aluminium twinspar
- **SUSPENSION** "Upside-down" telescopic fork, single shock rising-rate rear
- **BRAKES** Twin carbon fibre discs front, single disc rear
- **WEIGHT** 130kg (287lb)
- **TOP SPEED** 298km/h (185mph)

GRAND PRIX RIDING STYLES

Geoff Duke was known for his elegant style, in part determined by the racing tyres of his era.

Italian rider Tarquinio Provini was famous for his "chin-on-the-tank" riding style.

The evolution of the Grand Prix racing motorcycle has been mirrored by corresponding refinement in riding techniques. Improved handling on modern bikes, allows today's racers to make full use of the machines' acceleration.

The enormous power and wide tyres of modern machines encourage riders to hang off the bike when cornering.

Fuel tank breather

Carbon-fibre brakes are most effective when they are hot. In very cold or wet conditions, covers are used

34 is Kevin Schwantz's lucky racing number

Radiator

The low frontal area keeps wind resistance down, aiding acceleration and maximizing the top speed.

Slick racing tyre

The alloy wheels have hollow spokes

The fairing is made from lightweight, Kevlar-reinforced carbon fibre

Superbikes

Superbike racing originated in America, but has spread to the rest of the world. A World Championship for the class has been in existence since 1988. The rules of superbike racing demand that the motorcycles must look like models that can be bought for ordinary use on the road – a policy that keeps costs down, as well as making the events interesting for spectators. Competition is fierce, and the races are spectacular. Superbike racing has been a stepping stone for many Grand Prix riders: American World Champions Freddie Spencer, Eddie Lawson, and Wayne Rainey all graduated to Grand Prix racing from superbikes.

Wayne Rainey won the 1983 American Superbike Championship on this Kawasaki. He switched to the Honda team and won again in 1987, before winning three 500cc world championships for Yamaha.

1983 Kawasaki ZX750
While a typical racing superbike may closely resemble a production machine, many parts are upgraded and improved to make the bikes faster and lighter. Superbikes are designed to have the best possible handling under racing conditions. This Kawasaki ZX750 was raced by Wayne Rainey in 1983.

Special fasteners allow the bodywork to be removed quickly

Gas reservoir for rear shock absorber

Reshaped seat prevents the rider sliding backwards under acceleration

The box-section alloy swingarm is stronger and lighter than a standard component

Competition dry clutch assembly

Honda rider Fred Merkel won the first two World Superbike Championships in 1989 and again in 1990, but since then Ducati have dominated the class. This is in part because the rules of the championship limit four-cylinder bikes to 750cc, whereas two-cylinder machines are allowed to have a capacity of up to 1000cc. As a direct result, the Ducati 888 V-twins have been given a distinct advantage in this championship.

Instrument pod

The bodywork is the same as for Kawasaki's road bike

Oil cooler is located behind the perforated number plate

Ignition coils

Electronic ignition sender

Lightweight three-spoke alloy wheels. Keeping unsprung weight low is a priority

THE DAYTONA 200

The Daytona 200, America's most famous road race, was first run in 1937 and has always been fiercely contested. Although designated a road race, the original course ran along the beach of the famous Florida resort. The race moved to a purpose-built track in 1961 and has been run to Superbike rules for specification machines since 1985.

Although the Daytona 200-mile race does not form part of the World Championship, it is probably the most prestigious single Superbike race in the world. On the banked track machines can achieve impressive speeds. The race takes place in March and traditionally heralds the start of the international racing season.

SPECIFICATIONS

Kawasaki ZX750

- **ENGINE** Double overhead-camshaft in-line four cylinder
- **BORE AND STROKE** 66 x 54mm (2⅜ x 2⅛in)
- **CAPACITY** 738cc
- **POWER OUTPUT** Not measured
- **CARBURATION** Four 34mm Mikuni
- **IGNITION** Electronic
- **TRANSMISSION** Five-speed gearbox, chain drive
- **CLUTCH** Dry multiplate
- **FRAME** Tubular cradle
- **SUSPENSION** Telescopic forks front, cantilever rear
- **BRAKES** Double discs front, single disc rear
- **WEIGHT** 219kg (483lb)
- **TOP SPEED** 257km/h (160mph) (estimated)
- **YEAR OF CONSTRUCTION** 1983

Endurance Racing

ENDURANCE EVENTS ARE a severe test of man and machine, as races last for up to 24 hours. To win, a team must cover the greatest possible distance within the allotted time limit. A machine's reliability is as vital as its speed; the need for regular stops for fuel, oil, and tyre changes means that races can be won and lost on pit stops. Two or three riders take turns to pilot the bikes, and even after 24 hours of racing, positions can be decided by margins of only a few seconds. If a machine is crashed, or breaks down on the circuit, the rider must push it back to the pits, without assistance, before repairs can be carried out. The most famous Endurance race is the Bol d'Or event in France, which first took place in 1922.

In a "Le Mans"-style start (as above at Le Mans), riders run across the race track, and start their machines when the flag drops.

The large capacity fuel tank has a quick-opening cap

1971 Triumph Trident
In 1971, Triumph won the gruelling Bol d'Or for the second year running. The event was held on the famous Bugatti circuit at Le Mans. Team riders Ray Pickrell and Percy Tait completed 616 laps on the Triumph Trident seen below, at an average speed of 114km/h (71mph).

Ergonomic tank- and seat-design are essential as riders spend long periods on the track

Rear light and number plate

Cover for battery in seat hump

Crankcase breather pipe

In the early 1970s, endurance racers used road tyres

The rear wheel must be easily removable for rapid pit stop tyre changes

Three-into-one exhaust system

Twelve hours into the 1992 Le Mans 24-hour race, Terry Rymer races toward a team win for Kawasaki. Lap times hardly drop during the night.

TRIUMPH

The headlights are angled to give maximum visibility when cornering or braking

Fast pitwork is crucial to the team's success. Here, the Godier-Genoud team takes on more fuel during the 1977 Bol d'Or.

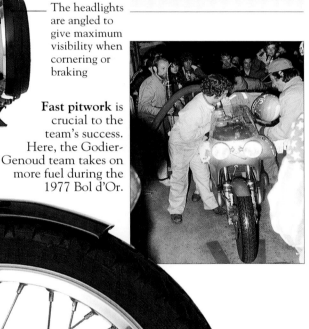

70

A light above the racing number, assists the pit crew and the scorers recording lap times

Brake pads often need to be changed during the race

Twin cast-iron discs

TT Racing

The coveted Tourist Trophy

RACING ON PUBLIC ROADS is banned on mainland Britain, so when English enthusiasts wanted to stage a road race they decided on the Isle of Man. The Tourist Trophy races started in 1907, and still are the most famous and demanding in the world. The natural obstacles of the road circuit made it very dangerous, and in 1977 it lost its status as a World Championship event. The TT is still an enormously popular festival.

The landmarks of the TT course have changed very little over the years, though the road surface has improved. The Quarter Bridge Hotel (above) still stands, and riders now have to negotiate a roundabout at this particular corner.

The "Mountain Course" is 37.7 miles (60.7km) long and includes 264 corners. This course was first used in 1911 when Oliver Godfrey won the Senior race at an average of 47.63mph (76.65km/h) on an Indian. Eighty years later the track surface has improved, but it still follows the same route. The lap record now stands at 18 minutes 18.8 seconds; an average of 123.61mph (198.9km/h).

RAMSEY •
The Hairpin •
• Gooseneck
• KIRK MICHAEL
• Verandah
• Ballacraine
• Windy Corner
• Creg-ny-Baa
CROSBY •
• Governor's Bridge
Quarter Bridge • • DOUGLAS

1938 Manx Norton

Norton are one of the most successful makers in the history of the TT race. In 1907 Rem Fowler won the twin-cylinder race at the very first TT. Eighty-five years later Steve Hislop, riding a Norton rotary, won the Senior race. Between these years were another 19 Senior, and 12 Junior TT victories. Their most famous and successful racers were the overhead-camshaft singles that first made their island debut in 1927 and achieved their last victory in 1961. They were known as Manx Nortons because of their success on the island course.

Megaphone exhaust

SPECIFICATIONS

Norton Manx 500

- **ENGINE** Overhead-camshaft single
- **BORE AND STROKE** 79 x 100mm (3 x 4in)
- **CAPACITY** 490cc
- **POWER OUTPUT** 35bhp (estimated)
- **CARBURATION** Amal with remote float bowl
- **IGNITION** Racing magneto
- **TRANSMISSION** Four-speed, chain drive
- **CLUTCH** Dry multiplate
- **FRAME** Tubular cradle
- **SUSPENSION** Girder forks, plunger rear
- **BRAKES** Single drum front and rear
- **WEIGHT** 380lb (172kg) (estimated)
- **TOP SPEED** 110mph (177km/h)
- **YEAR OF CONSTRUCTION** 1938

Governor's Bridge is the last of the track's many corners. From here there is a flat out dash to the finishing line.

The first three celebrate after the 1938 Senior. Harold Daniell (centre) won, from Stanley Woods (left), and Freddie Frith.

Harold Daniell rode Nortons to victory in the Senior TT three times. As well as the 1938 race he also won in 1947 and 1949.

A souvenir badge may be all that some Isle of Man TT visitors take away with them, after two weeks of racing, practice, and events.

Stone guard

Steve Hislop in the 1992 Senior at Creg-ny-Baa on his way to Norton's first TT win for 19 years.

Norton

Girder forks were used on the TT race machines. Telescopic forks replaced them on works bikes from 1938

The overhead-camshaft engine was available in 350 and 500cc capacities

Motocross

THE IDEA OF RACING motorcycles around a field, through mud, and over bumps is not attributable to any one place or time, but certainly the sport of "scrambling" first appeared in Britain in the nineteen twenties. International competition began after the Second World War as the "Moto-Cross des Nations", and a European championship for individual riders first took place in 1952 – this became the World Championship in 1957. The sport has become very popular in America, where the national championship is known as "Super Cross". In America some events are staged on floodlit artificial tracks created in stadiums.

Motocross riders start the event lined-up across the track. The race for the first corner, and an early lead, is frantic.

1992 Husqvarna Motocross TC610

The critical component of a motocross bike is its suspension, which must isolate the rider from bumps and keep the rear wheel on the ground, as an airborne wheel cannot transmit power. This Husqvarna has 280-300mm (11-12in) of suspension travel at the front and at the rear. The bike is built for the increasingly popular four-stroke class, although most Grand Prix machines are two strokes.

Bracing strengthens the handlebars

Motocrossers are often equipped with hand protectors

The seat is long to allow for a variety of riding positions

Flexible mudguards are less likely to suffer crash damage

"Upside-down" forks

Radiator ducts

Plastic guards protect fork sliders

Pedals and foot rests fold up to prevent crash damage

Long-travel suspension keeps the tyre on the track and the rider on the bike

SPECIFICATIONS

Husqvarna TC610

- **ENGINE** Double-overhead-camshaft water-cooled single cylinder
- **BORE AND STROKE** 98 x 76.5mm (3⅞ x 3in)
- **CAPACITY** 577cc
- **POWER OUTPUT** 50bhp (estimated)
- **CARBURATION** Dell'Orto carbs
- **IGNITION** Electronic
- **TRANSMISSION** Six-speed gearbox, chain drive
- **CLUTCH** Wet multiplate
- **FRAME** Tubular cradle
- **SUSPENSION** Telescopic forks, rear swingarm single shock with rising rate linkage
- **BRAKES** Discs front and rear
- **WEIGHT** 117kg (258lb)
- **TOP SPEED** Dependent on gearing
- **YEAR OF CONSTRUCTION** 1993

Tracks offer different riding conditions. The British Grand Prix venue at Hawkstone Park is famous for its long hill (above) and sandy ground.

CLOTHING

Motocross is a physically demanding sport. The rider's clothing must provide maximum protection without impeding his movement or making him excessively hot. Good ventilation is crucial.

- Ventilated crash helmet
- Goggles
- Gloves designed to grip in all conditions
- Ventilated synthetic shirt
- Strong boots provide ankle support and shin protection
- Knee protection must allow flexibility
- Smooth-soled boots
- Body armour
- Reinforced motocross jeans

Lifting handle

Kill button

Motocross bikes are exceptionally tall. The saddle height is just under 1 metre (39in).

Lightweight exhaust system

Alloy swingarm

Knobbly tyres transmit maximum power to the ground

The disc brakes must be very sensitive to avoid locking the wheels on loose surfaces

Plastic disc guard

Spectacular jumps are part of motocross, as a flying KTM (see also p.134) demonstrates.

Trials

Modern trials bikes make almost any terrain passable. Here, Diego Bosis climbs a rock face.

O NE OF THE OLDEST FORMS of motorcycle sport, trials were originally devised as a test of machinery. The increasing reliability and performance of motorcycles turned events into a test of the riders' skills in surmounting a series of obstacles. Events are split into observed sections; a penalty point is deducted for coming to a standstill, and a maximum of five points for failing to complete the section at all, or within the time limit. Trials events enjoy huge popularity as a participation sport, riders graduate from club events to National and World Championship competition. The Scottish Six Days Trial, established in 1910, attracts hundreds of competitors – from club riders to professionals – but this demanding event is not included in the World Championship.

1964 Bultaco Sherpa
The Bultaco Sherpa is the basis of the modern trials bike. Before the appearance of the Bultaco, the sport was dominated by large-capacity, heavyweight, four-stroke singles; this prototype, developed by Sammy Miller and ridden by him to many international wins, began the almost complete takeover of the sport by two-stroke machines.

The air filter intake is positioned under the seat to prevent water penetration

High-level exhaust pipe with heat guard

Sammy Miller scored many trials wins for Ariel before moving to Bultaco (pp.140-41) in the 1965 season. He later developed innovative trials bikes for Honda and, in 40 years, won over a thousand trials events, including five Scottish Six Days Trials.

Serrated metal footrests

As speed is unimportant, gearing of the bike is very low

Lightweight aluminium alloy brake hub

SPECIFICATIONS

1964 Bultaco Sherpa
- **ENGINE** Single cylinder two-stroke
- **BORE AND STROKE** 2¹³⁄₁₆ x 2⅜in (72 x 60mm)
- **CAPACITY** 244cc
- **POWER OUTPUT** 19.5bhp
- **CARBURATION** IRZ carburettor
- **IGNITION** Femsa generator and coil
- **TRANSMISSION** Four-speed gearbox, chain drive
- **CLUTCH** Wet multiplate
- **FRAME** Tubular cradle
- **SUSPENSION** Telescopic forks, rear swingarm
- **BRAKES** Bultaco drum front and rear
- **WEIGHT** 92.5kg (204lb)
- **TOP SPEED** Not assessed
- **YEAR OF CONSTRUCTION** 1964

New Zealander Steve Merriman prepares to drop his Aprilia into a rocky crevasse during the 1992 Irish World Trials.

INTERNATIONAL SIX DAYS ENDURO

Enduro competitions are off-road races against the clock. Arriving late or early for a checkpoint incurs a penalty but timed enduro sections are not observed, as in trials. Riders also perform special tests: riding from a standing start, or replacing rear tyres against the clock.

The most important single event is the International Six Days Enduro, first held in 1913, and until 1984 known as the International Six Days Trial. Teams from different countries compete for medals over six gruelling days of competition.

The design of trials bikes has evolved to survive all weather and ground conditions. `

Enduro motorbikes must be road legal. Headlights are compulsory.

Off-road riders often use a "foot down" cornering technique, as above.

Narrow, small-capacity fuel tank

The steering-head angle is steep to give increased manoeuvrability

Lightweight aluminium mudguards

The knobbly tyres are run at low pressure to increase grip

Radially finned cylinder head

A bash plate protects the engine and frame rails from rocky ground

Speedometer drive

The 53cm (21in) front wheel makes climbing over obstacles easier

Speedway

THIS FAST AND SPECTACULAR SPORT originated in America in 1902, was refined in Australia, and came to Europe in the late 1920s. Speedway bikes have no brakes, and riders must slow down by sliding the machines through turns. Races are run anti-clockwise on quarter-mile (402m) oval dirt tracks, four riders compete over four laps; the right foot rest is set low, but the left side is high and further forward to prevent it hitting the track. Each race lasts about one minute; the races often take place at night under floodlights. Speedway meetings are a contest between two teams, with two riders from each team taking part in each race. The most points accrued decides the winning team.

A good start is crucial. The rider who leads at the first corner has a big advantage.

American rider Bruce Penhall won the 1981 World Speedway Championship on the bike seen below, with its cover.

A silencer is fitted. As many speedway tracks are in built-up areas, noise regulations are strict

1981 Weslake Speedway
All racing bikes evolve to suit their sport, but few are more specialised than speedway machines. Their basic appearance has not altered since the 1940s, though many details have changed. Weslake bikes dominated speedway in the late seventies and early eighties.

The fuel tank holds enough methanol to last four laps

A coloured disc hides a conventional spoked wheel

The carburettor is covered by a protective shroud

Oil in frame tube

Oil pump

The **rider** controls the slide using the handlebars, throttle, and his body weight.

Minimal handlebar controls operate clutch and throttle. There is no gearbox

Forks are steeply angled giving more responsive steering and improved handling in the slide

THE SPORT OF ICE RACING

Ice racing is a very popular winter pursuit in Scandinavia, Poland, Russia, and other countries that have cold climates. The ice track used is oval, and the bikes are very like those used in speedway racing.

To achieve a better grip on the ice, tyres are fitted with hundreds of steel spikes, allowing the riders to achieve dramatic cornering angles. Riders strap sections of old tyres to their left knees for protection when cornering. Most ice bikes are physically bigger than speedway machines and have a two-speed gearbox.

A protective guard encloses the steel spikes of the tyre.

The telescopic front forks allow little movement. There is no rear suspension

SPECIFICATIONS

Weslake Speedway
- **ENGINE** Air-cooled four-valve single cylinder
- **BORE AND STROKE** 3¹⁄₁₆ x 3⅜in (80 x 85.9mm)
- **CAPACITY** 500cc
- **POWER OUTPUT** 48bhp
- **CARBURATION** 1⅜in (34mm) Amal
- **IGNITION** Interspan electronic
- **TRANSMISSION** No gearbox – gearing is changed according to track conditions
- **CLUTCH** Multiplate dry
- **FRAME** Open cradle with stressed engine
- **SUSPENSION** Telescopic forks
- **BRAKES** None
- **WEIGHT** 183lb (83kg)
- **TOP SPEED** 60-80mph (97-128km/h) The speeds achieved depend on the track conditions and the gearing used.
- **YEAR OF CONSTRUCTION** 1981
- Highly-combustible Methanol is the alcohol-based fuel used for speedway bikes.

The front wheel is much larger in diameter than the rear and carries a narrower tyre

DID YOU KNOW?
New Zealander Ivan Mauger is the world's most successful speedway rider. He won six World Championships, four World Team Cups, two World Pairs Championships, and three World Long Track titles between 1968 and 1979.

Desert Racing

FIRST HELD IN 1979, the Paris-Dakar rally was conceived by Frenchman Thierry Sabine. The race is a gruelling 15,000 kilometres (9,320 miles), which only 10-25% of entrants finish. Each day riders must complete a stage of between 400 and 1200 kilometres (between 248 and 746 miles), it takes about three weeks to complete the course most of which is over desert terrain. There are some similar competitions, but the Paris-Dakar race is still the longest and toughest.

In the 1991 Paris-Dakar, British rider John Watson-Miller was forced to retire 3 days from the finish after breaking both his feet.

1990 Honda XRV750
Honda built eight machines to contest the 1991 Paris Dakar. Only two of them completed the course. This one failed to finish after its rider, John Watson-Miller, was injured three days' ride from the finish. The "Marathon" class in which they are entered allows the use of lightly-modified production machines with changes permitted only to the tank, rear shock absorber, and exhaust system. Long-distance competitions have a dedicated following in Spain, France, and Italy, where there is a big market for replicas of this type of machine.

The air intake is positioned to stop sand getting into it

The Honda is dominated by its huge fuel tank

A computerized compass is mounted in a slot behind the seat

Additional rear fuel tank

The tyres are filled with puncture-resisting mousse

A plastic shield protects the rear disc

Tool box

The bash plate protects the bottom of the engine

Navigation is a major problem in the featureless desert terrain, shown left, as getting lost can be fatal. Riders must find the finishing points of each stage for themselves, no outside assistance is permitted during the race, although riders can help one another. Competitors often travel in small groups, as shown far left. Satellite navigation is banned, but all bikes carry sophisticated computerized compasses that continually calculate their position, as well as providing information on fuel reserves and the bike's average speed.

Long-distance riders stay in groups for mutual assistance and safety.

Gilera rider Luigino Medardo, competing in the 1991 Paris-Dakar race, negotiates a rutted track on his RC600.

Navigation notes are contained in the "Road Book"

A rear view of the Honda displays its massive height.

Long-travel suspension

Water tank

Factory riders change tyres regularly

The route of the rally changes each year. The route shown above was taken in 1991. In 1992, the final destination was Cape Town, rather than Dakar.

SPECIFICATIONS

Honda XRV750
- **ENGINE** Four-stroke 52° V-twin
- **BORE AND STROKE** 81 x 72mm
- **CAPACITY** 742cc
- **POWER OUTPUT** 59 bhp @ 5500 rpm
- **CARBURATION** Twin 36.5mm carbs.
- **IGNITION** Electric ignition
- **TRANSMISSION** Five-speed gearbox, chain drive
- **CLUTCH** Seven-plate
- **FRAME** Duplex cradle
- **SUSPENSION** Air forks 220mm-travel front, monoshock air adjustable pro link, 210mm-travel rear
- **BRAKES** Two-piston single-disc front, single-piston single-disc rear
- **WEIGHT** 210kg (463lb)
- **TOP SPEED** 185km/h (115mph)
- **YEAR OF CONSTRUCTION** 1990

American Racing

Scott Parker looks for the opposition while cornering. He won the National Championship in 1988, 1989, and 1990.

MOTORCYCLE RACING IN AMERICA became established as a professional sport very quickly. In the early years of the twentieth century, promoters built banked, wooden, oval tracks, and offered generous prize money to attract top riders. The public flocked to watch the racing, and manufacturers profited from the sports' popularity. Unfortunately board-track racing was very dangerous and, after a series of horrific accidents to riders, the popularity of the sport declined. Dirt-track racing then became the most popular motorcycle sport in America. Races took place over mile (1.6km) and half-mile (800m) ovals or on a TT-style course featuring left turns and jumps. A national championship was first run in 1954, and included road-racing events. The same machine was required to be ridden in all events, and a rugged, versatile machine-design evolved, which shaped American production motorcycles.

1972 Harley-Davidson XR 750
In 1968, a change in the rules of American dirt-track racing allowed the use of overhead-valve 750cc engines. Harley-Davidson then produced a new iron-barrelled motor in response – the XR 750. It was extensively redesigned and improved for the 1972 season and became an American motorcycle classic. This example, ridden by Mark Brelsford, won the American Motorcycle Association Championship in 1972.

Large air filters prevent any dirt being sucked into the engine, without impairing performance

Small-capacity fuel tank – races are rarely more than 25 miles (40km) long

Rear brake reservoir

Brake pedal

Gearchange

Screws fix the tyres to the rims to prevent movement

Motor Oils were manufactured under licence by the Sun Oil Company to Harley's own specification.

DESERT RACING IN AMERICA

Desert racing is popular in America. The Baja Desert (above) is often used for these cross-country events.

Hundreds of riders gather at a massed start of a race (above), held in the 1950s; various types of machines took part in these amateur races.

Mark Brelsford rode with the racing number 87 in 1972 and won the champion's number 1 plate for the 1973 season

Italian Ceriani forks

Oil cooler

No front brake is fitted to the hub for oval-track events

Ricky Graham makes a leap on an XR750 in the course of a TT-style race.

Riders pitch their bikes into the corners of the oval tracks at over 100mph (160km/h).

The flanged alloy rim gives the wheel additional strength despite its lightweight construction

Tyres are cut by hand with razor blades, a knife, or an electric cutting tool, to suit different track conditions

SPECIFICATIONS

Harley-Davidson XR750
- **ENGINE** Overhead-valve 45° V-twin
- **BORE AND STROKE** 3⅛ x 3in (79 x 76mm)
- **CAPACITY** 750cc (45cu. in)
- **POWER OUTPUT** 90+ bhp
- **CARBURATION** Two Mikuni carburettors
- **IGNITION** Magneto
- **TRANSMISSION** Four-speed gearbox, chain drive
- **CLUTCH** Wet multiplate
- **FRAME** Tubular cradle
- **SUSPENSION** Telescopic forks, rear swingarm
- **BRAKES** No front brakes, single disc rear
- **WEIGHT** 295lb (134kg)
- **TOP SPEED** 130mph (209km/h)
- **YEAR OF CONSTRUCTION** 1972

Drag Racing

Even the huge slicks fitted to top dragsters struggle for grip when subjected to 400bhp of abuse.

I N DRAG RACING, TWO RIDERS COMPETE over a quarter-mile (402m) straight track. Race meetings take the form of a series of elimination heats continuing until an outright winner emerges. Competitors are split into classes according to type of machine and the fuel used. Bikes vary from production bikes to vast twin-engined supercharged machines that run on methanol and nitro methane. Drag racing originated on the wide, straight roads of America, but has spread worldwide. A European variation exists, called "sprinting", in which a single rider races against the clock.

1977 Kawasaki 2400cc Dragster
The elemental characteristics of a drag racer are simple: maximum power is allied to minimum weight. Power output can easily be doubled or even trebled by the simple expedient of adding more engines. The vital function of transmitting power to the track is performed by an extremely wide rear tyre. Because enormous power output is required, the engines do not survive for long, and are usually rebuilt after each race meeting. This particular dragster was built by Jan Smit and raced by the Dutch rider Henk Vink.

Harley-Davidson engines have always been a favourite choice for American drag racers. The machine raced by successful American drag rider Marion Owens (right) uses two of them.

Rear wheel cover with air-brushed flame paintwork and identification number

Under extreme acceleration the rider is forced back against the "bumstop"

The frame is heavily braced to prevent flexing

The rear cylinders are reversed to keep the distance between inlet tracts as short as possible

Inlet manifold

The fastest time for a single run, over a quarter of a mile (402m) from a standing start, is 7.08 seconds by American Bo O'Brechta, riding a 1200cc Kawasaki in 1980.

Wheelie bars

Slick tyre

Henk Vink, on an earlier, single-engined bike, is already pulling clear of the opposition, Britain's John Hobbs.

The tank holds just enough nitro-methane for one race

The upper frame rails are padded to provide greater comfort for the prone rider

Dragsters have "wheelie bars" at the back, to prevent the front wheel from lifting too high under acceleration.

Foot controls are positioned to the rear of the bike

The wheelbase is exceptionally long.

The bike's half-fairing is lavishly decorated with airbrush painting

Raked forks give the bike stability in a straight line

The supercharger compresses the fuel mixture, increasing the power of the engine

Hilborn fuel injector supplies the mixture

SPECIFICATIONS

Kawasaki Dragster
- **ENGINE** Two double-overhead-camshaft in-line four-cylinder engines
- **BORE AND STROKE** Not measured
- **CAPACITY** 2400cc
- **POWER OUTPUT** Over 400 bhp
- **CARBURATION** Fuel injector
- **IGNITION** Lucas magneto
- **TRANSMISSION** B & J transmission
- **CLUTCH** Four-plate slide clutch
- **FRAME** Purpose-built tubular steel cradle
- **SUSPENSION** Telescopic front forks, no rear suspension
- **BRAKES** Double disc front brakes, single rear disc brake
- **WEIGHT** Not measured
- **TOP SPEED** 300km/h (186mph)
- **YEAR OF CONSTRUCTION** 1977

Sidecar Racing

Sidecars were originally added to motorcycles to increase their load-carrying capacity, a fact that did not stop people racing them. By the 1950s, racing sidecars had evolved from being bikes with chairs bolted on, into integrated structures: Grand Prix machines now have more in common with racing cars than with motorbikes. The driver and passenger of the outfit work together as a team; the passenger adjusts his weight to control wheelspin and help gain traction. Machine, driver, and passenger work together in a subtle three-way collaboration.

Four times World Champion Steve Webster pictured with passenger Gavin Simmons.

Terry Vinnicombe and partner John Flaxman head for victory in the 1968 750cc Sidecar TT.

Ignition is constant loss

Passenger grab-rail

Square section tyre

The all-enclosing fairing is designed to reduce drag. The passenger lies face down in the "chair" on the long straights.

Red and white colours are used by the sponsor Tom Kirby

1968 Kirby BSA Racing Sidecar
British race regulations allowed engines bigger than the 500cc limit imposed on Grand Prix machines. This 750cc BSA-powered outfit won the 1968 Sidecar TT.

The fairing hides the front wheel and suspension

Clear perspex passenger windscreen

Rev counter

Leading-link forks are used. Telescopic forks are not strong enough

The sidecar's knee troughs caused them to be called "kneelers"

Two exhaust pipes project well clear of the frame

Gearchange pedal

This overhead view clearly shows the sidecar rider's saddle and knee troughs, and the passenger's exposed platform.

SIDECAR MOTOCROSS

Most motorcycle races include a class for sidecars but few compet-itions are more physically punish-ing than sidecar motocross events.

Motocross right- and left-handed chairs need different riding styles to take this corner. Passengers move their weight to keep outfits tightly in to the corner (right and above right).

DID YOU KNOW?

With more rubber in contact with the road, sidecars can often corner faster than solo machines, but their poorer power-to-weight ratio makes them accelerate more slowly. On some tracks, sidecars can be faster than solo machines.

SPECIFICATIONS

Kirby BSA Sidecar Outfit
- **ENGINE** Standard BSA parallel twin
- **BORE AND STROKE** 75 x 74mm
- **CAPACITY** 654cc
- **POWER OUTPUT** 62bhp @ 7,000rpm
- **CARBURATION** Two Amal GP2 units (with remote float chambers)
- **IGNITION** Lucas 12-volt twin coil
- **TRANSMISSION** Four-speed gearbox, chain drive
- **CLUTCH** Multiplate
- **FRAME** One-off steel duplex cradle-type, based on the Manx Norton frame (p.71)
- **SUSPENSION** Leading-link Earles-type forks, rear swingarm with Girling dampers
- **BRAKES** Hydraulic single disc front, hydraulic rear drum
- **WEIGHT** 430lb (195kg)
- **TOP SPEED** 115mph (185km/h)
- **YEAR OF CONSTRUCTION** 1968

The rider crouches over the exposed engine and carburettors

Glass-fibre wheel guard

60

Outfits slide when cornering and so the tyres of the sidecar get very hard use

What Makes a Motorcycle?

MOTORCYCLES ALL HAVE two wheels and an engine but vary infinitely, from mopeds to Grand Prix racers. Yet the biggest and the smallest machines are built in the same way; a piston engine and telescopic forks are used almost universally. After a hundred years motorcycles are still essentially similar.

Four-stroke Engines

THE BASIC PRINCIPLE OF THIS efficient engine remains the same after 100 years of development. Petrol and air enter a sealed cylinder; the combustible gas mixture is compressed by the piston and ignited. The resultant explosion causes the gas to expand, forcing the piston down. The crankshaft converts the downward motion into circular motion. The sequence is known as "Suck, Squeeze, Bang, Blow".

Inlet valve opens

Exhaust valve closed

Piston moves down

Fuel/air mixture is sucked into the cylinder

1. The induction stroke (Suck)

Inlet valve closes

Exhaust valve closed

Piston moves up

Fuel/air mixture is compressed

2. The compression stroke (Squeeze)

Inlet valve closed

Exhaust valve closed

Fuel/air mixture is ignited

Exploding gas expands forcing the piston down

3. The power stroke (Bang)

Inlet valve closed

Exhaust valve opens

Piston rises

Spent charge (exhaust gas) is forced out

4. The exhaust stroke (Blow)

Velocette OHV Engine
Traditional four-stroke designs were simple and economical, but to increase power, engines needed more power strokes. This required faster revving engines, faster gas exchange, and reciprocating parts of minimum weight. This criteria led engine design toward light alloy, multi-cylinder, multi-valve engines with overhead camshafts.

Cylinder head

Inlet port connects to the carburettor

Cam followers

Magneto drive

Camshaft gear

Oil passageway

Oil pump

The circular motion of the crankshaft reaches the wheels via the transmission system (pp.176-7)

Exhaust port

Valve lifter

The Camshaft

Engine breathing is controlled by the camshaft. The valves open once for every two engine revolutions, so the camshaft rotates at half engine speed, driven by belt, chain, or gear from the crankshaft (see diagram). When the valves open and close, and how much they open, has a major effect on engine performance. Modern engines have separate exhaust and inlet camshafts mounted on top of the cylinder head, allowing a higher rev range. Shown here is a Yamaha FZR1000 inlet camshaft. Each of the three inlet valves has a camshaft lobe.

Raised lobes push the valves open as the camshaft turns

Bearing surfaces

Lubrication holes

Drive sprocket mounting

Camshaft follower

The Cylinder Head

Modern engines use several small valves, rather than two big valves, to allow for maximum gas flow and minimum component weight. Combustion occurs at the cylinder head, making it the hottest part of the engine. It must be cooled and there must be provision for lubrication of the valve gear and camshafts. Modern engines are liquid cooled, allowing more precise tolerances and quieter running.

Shown below is the pistons' view of the cylinder-head

Valve

Except for Desmodromic Ducati engines (pp.92-5), the valve is closed by a spring. At 10,000 rpm the valves must open and close 5,000 times in one minute. The gap between the camshaft and the valve opening mechanism, is critical for effective gas-flow.

Valve spring keeps valve shut

Valve

Sealing lip

Fixing-stud hole

Cavity for camshaft-drive chain

Exhaust port

Water passageway

Oil passageway

Spark plug hole

Water passageway

Valve guide

Inlet port

The Piston

Pistons are usually made from a light aluminium alloy, because of alloy's lightweight and thermal-efficient properties. For maximum efficiency, piston rings ensure a good seal between the piston and the bore. These hard metal rings sit in grooves around the piston, preventing compression leakage to the crankcase, and oil escaping from the crankcase to the upper cylinder.

Piston crown

Compression ring

Scraper ring

Oil-control ring

Piston skirt

Lubrication and thermal expansion slot

The diagram *right, shows the basic relationship between the essential reciprocating components in an overhead camshaft engine. The camshaft-drive pulleys must be geared to allow the camshaft to turn at half crankshaft speed.*

Camshaft

Timing belt or chain connects crank- and camshafts

Valve

Piston

Crankshaft

Two-stroke Engines

A TWO-STROKE ENGINE in its most basic form has only three moving parts: the crankshaft, the connecting rod, and the piston, making it cheap to manufacture. Because it fires every two strokes, the engine gives a power stroke every revolution, so the potential power output is high. As the crankcases are used in the combustion process and cannot carry lubricant, moving parts are lubricated by oil in the fuel. This means that oil is burnt off during combustion, making two-stroke exhaust dirtier than a four stroke's.

Radiator

Exhaust ports

Expansion chamber

Silencer

Two-stroke Operation

Although mechanically simple, the operation of the two-stroke is complex. Unlike a four stroke, the piston performs three different functions; it is important to recognize the separate roles of the top, sides, and the bottom of the piston. It controls the flow of gases, so in its most basic form the two stroke has no mechanical valves, simply ports that are open or closed dependent on the position of the piston. The example shown here is an old fashioned three-port engine, but the principle remains the same on a modern engine. The ports on a two stroke are cut into the cylinder bore, wearing piston and bore more quickly than a four stroke.

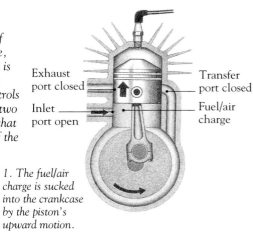

Exhaust port closed

Inlet port open

Transfer port closed

Fuel/air charge

1. The fuel/air charge is sucked into the crankcase by the piston's upward motion.

Exhaust port open

Inlet port closed

Transfer port open

Charge enters chamber

2. The piston's downward motion forces the fuel/air charge into the combustion chamber.

Charge is compressed

Exhaust port closed

Inlet port open

Transfer port closed

3. The piston's upward motion compresses the charge in the combustion chamber.

Charge ignites

Exhaust port closed

Inlet port open

Transfer port closed

Piston forced downward

4. The spark plug ignites the charge, causing an explosion that forces the piston down.

Motion of the crankshaft is continued

Exhaust forced out

Exhaust port open

Inlet port closed

Transfer port open

Fresh charge

5. A new charge, forced upward by the piston, expels the exhaust, and the whole process repeats.

Exhaust First

The tuning of two-stroke engines is one of the esoteric arts of motorcycle design: maximum power is achieved through the use of strangely shaped exhaust pipes called "expansion chambers". Four-stroke engines require an exhaust of a specifically 'tuned' length, but two strokes are unique in the extent that they depend on its design. The slightest variation in the shape and volume of the pipe can have a massive affect on the engine's performance.

The Standard Two-stroke
Firing every revolution, two-strokes run hotter than a four-stroke. The cooling fin area on an air-cooled engine is very large. Engines have an optimum functioning temperature so high performance machines usually adopt water cooling to keep temperature constant.

REED VALVE
Extended inlet port opening times allow maximum crankcase filling. This results in high crankcase pressure, and can result in "blow back" through the carburettor. A non-return reed valve, such as the one shown here, can prevent this, allowing mixture to flow into the engine, but not to escape.

Disc-valve Engines
The piston usually governs the inlet port timing of a two-stroke, but some engines use a rotary disc valve. The valve is controlled by the crankshaft, with the carburettor mounted directly onto the side of the crankcase.

Rotary disc-valve

THE WANKEL ROTARY ENGINE
Invented by Felix Wankel in the 1950's, the rotary theoretically offers advantages of a lightweight engine with high power output and minimal vibration. A three-sided rotor turns inside an eccentrically shaped chamber, allowing the four combustion processes to take place at the same time, without the power-sapping stop/start of a reciprocating piston as it travels up and down a cylinder. However, the potential of the rotary engine has never been fully realized; Norton are the only manufacturer to have persevered with it.

MAIN COMPONENTS

Power-valve Engines
Power valves allow the shape of the exhaust port to be altered to provide optimum performance at a variety of different throttle openings. Most are electronically controlled in conjunction with the ignition timing.

ROTARY NORTON RACER NRS588
The Rotary Nortons have been successfully raced in the British Championship. Steve Hislop also won the 1992 Senior TT at the Isle of Man on a rotary Norton.

Carburation & Ignition

THE EXPLOSIVE CHARGE used in an internal combustion engine is a vapourised mixture of petrol and air. The ratio at which the two components are mixed is vital for the machine to perform effectively throughout its operating rev range. The carburettor controls the ratio and amount of the petrol/air mixture allowed to pass into the engine, at any given throttle position. The ignition system controls the timing of the spark that ignites the explosive charge. The timing of the explosion is critical: the faster the engine is running the earlier it must take place.

—— FUEL INJECTION ——
Fuel injection offers the potential of more efficient mixing and burning of fuel, giving better performance, economy, and reduced emissions. Modern systems are computer controlled. It has only recently been fitted to motorcycles in any quantity.

The Carburettor

Carburettors work on the "Venturi effect" (see diagram, right). This means that air is drawn through the carburettor, basically a large tube or "Venturi", by the sucking action of the pistons. As the air rushes into the engine it passes across a small hole at the bottom of the Venturi. This opening is connected to a reservoir of petrol that is sucked up and vapourized by the fast-moving air stream. A needle sits in the hole to regulate the petrol flow, operated either from the throttle cable, or by utilizing the engine's vacuum.

Needle to control petrol flow

Cable- or vacuum-operated slider controls air-flow

Air flow

Fuel/air mixture

Venturi or tube

Fuel reservoir or "float chamber"

The Venturi carburettor

The shape of the needle controls fuel-flow at small throttle openings

Vacuum chamber

Cable stop

Cold-start operating bar

Float chamber

Butterfly throttle valve

Fuel supply pipes

Full-throttle setting with butterflies and needles fully open

Slow-running adjuster

A row of four constant vacuum-carburettors, one for each cylinder. This is the view looking directly down the venturis. A "butterfly" throttle valve controls the air flow.

Adjusting screw
for points gap

Adjusting screw
for ignition timing

Lubrication
pad

Pivot

Heel for cam

Eccentric cam

Low tension
lead

Rubber seal

Well-insulated
high-tension lead

Weatherproof
spark plug
connector cap

*High-tension leads have to carry at
least 20,000 volts; obviously they must
be well insulated. The insulation makes
them much thicker than ordinary 6- or
12-volt low-tension leads. HT leads
are also suppressed to prevent them
interfering with radio signals.*

Spark
plug

Sealing
ring

*Contacts (left)
must be clean and adjusted
correctly to ensure exact
timing of the spark.*

Contact-breaker Points

*The contact-breaker points
(above), are controlled by a cam
that opens the points at the crucial
moment in the pistons travel. The
points opening causes the coil to emit a high-voltage spark
which is transmitted to the spark plug via a high-tension
(H.T.) lead. A condenser is fitted in the L.T. circuit to
prevent a spark occuring across the points when they open.*

The Coil

*The spark at the spark plug
is upwards of 20,000 volts
and is produced by the coil.
The coil basically consists of
two separate windings of
wire. The first carries 12
volts through the coil to the
points, when they open, the
12-volt current is interrupted causing a large
(high-tension), voltage to be magnetically
induced in the second winding. This winding
connects to the spark plug; the high voltage
spark jumps the gap between the core and
casing of the spark plug, igniting the mixture.*

The Spark Plug

*The spark plug's body connects
to earth, and its insulated core,
usually copper, carries
the high voltage.
This voltage must
reach earth to
complete the
circuit, so it
jumps the gap
between the
core and the
earthing
electrode
in the form
of a spark.*

Porcelain
insulation

Thread connects
to cylinder-head

Insulated core

Earth electrode

— FUNCTION OF THE COMPONENTS —

12-volt supply to coil,
(low tension lead)

This diagram shows
the relationship
between the
carburettor and the
ignition system.
The coil is shown
twice, to illustrate
its two different
states of activity,
depending on
whether the points
are open or closed.

Battery

Earth

Primary
winding

Coil passive
(points closed)

Secondary
winding

Coil active
(points open)

Contact-
breaker
points

Condenser

Earth

20,000+ volts from
coil to spark plug,
(high tension lead)

Spark plug

Earth

Combustion

Air

Fuel

Fuel/air mixture

Force created
moves piston
down

Electronic ignition

*Contact-breaker points need
regular cleaning and resetting,
or replacement. Dirty, pitted,
or worn points are often the
cause of poor performance.
Solid state technology has
been developed to replace
points with a sealed digital
unit (above), that is
controlled by magnetic signals
from a maintenance-free
sensor in place of the points.*

Transmission

THE TRANSMISSION SYSTEM conveys power from the engine to the rear wheel. The system usually consists of a clutch, a gearbox, and a chain. The gearbox allows the engine to be used effectively, without stalling or over-revving. The clutch acts as a mechanical switch, completing or breaking the connection between engine and gearbox when the rider changes gear or stops. The transmission fitted to many early machines simply comprised a belt connecting a small pulley at the engine to a large one at the rear wheel. There was no clutch, so the bike could not stop with the engine still running, and no gearbox, limiting the use of the engine. A clutch meant bikes stopped smoothly, and made chains more suitable for final drive.

The driving controls fitted to all modern motorcycles have standardized controls. The gearchange is operated by the left foot, and the clutch by the left hand. However, in the past, British and Italian machines used a right-foot shift, while American bikes used a hand change until the 1950s. This Henderson (above), has two shift levers: one for the three forward gears, and one for reverse, (a popular option with sidecar drivers).

The Wet Clutch

Most motorcycles use a compact multiplate "wet" clutch. This consists of an inner drum connected to the gearbox, and an outer drum connected to the engine. Both drums rotate in oil, independently of one another, but about the same axis. The two are linked by two types of clutch plate. Fibre plates are keyed to turn with the outer drum, while "friction" plates are keyed to turn with the inner drum. The plates are forced together by springs mounted in a "pressure plate". Pulling the clutch lever relieves this pressure, allowing the drums to turn independently.

Raised "keys" lock fibre plates to outer drum

Fibre friction plate

Metal friction plate

Splined "keys" lock metal friction plates to inner drum

Outer clutch drum

Pressure plate

Straight-cut primary-drive gear

The clutch unit and the primary drive, transfer the power from the engine to the gearbox. The clutch unit shown above is gear-driven from the crankshaft.

DRY CLUTCH

In order to gain start-line advantage, racers severely abuse their clutches at the start of a race. Once away and moving, they only use the clutch for down-shifts.

Racing machines, such as the Yamaha shown below, often use a "dry" multiplate clutch, which operates in a similar way to a wet clutch but does not run in oil.

A dry clutch (above), is not subject to the power-sapping drag of oil. It is exposed, with vents for air-cooling. Dry clutches are easier to work on if plates need to be changed at the race track; another advantage is that material from the clutch plates cannot pollute the oil.

Air vents cool the exposed dry clutch

Gearbox

Most modern gearboxes are constant-mesh designs. Each of the gear ratios is provided by a pair of cogs, one fixed and one free. The fixed cog rotates at the same speed as the shaft to which it is attached, while the free cog rotates at the speed imposed by its partner. To engage a ratio, both cogs must be fixed to their shafts by locking a fixed cog to a free cog, using slots or raised "dogs" on their sides. The cogs are moved by forks, controlled by a selector drum attached to the gear pedal.

2nd gear

5th gear

3rd gear

4th gear

6th gear

1st gear

Input shaft takes power from the primary drive

Gear lever selector shaft

Shafts run in bearings

Copper oil feed pipe

Aluminium outer casing

The final drive sprocket is mounted on the output shaft

This gearbox has top gear selected

> — DID YOU KNOW? —
> Both of the manufacturers Honda and Moto Guzzi have made motorbikes fitted with semi-automatic gear boxes. Despite their advantages, sales of the bikes were poor. The Swedish firm Husqvarna built an automatic motocross bike, but it too was unpopular.

Chains

Chain drive is the most common type of final drive found on motorcycles. It is cheaper, uses less power, and affects the handling of the machine less than shaft drive. The main drawback is that it requires more maintenance.

A modern "O Ring" chain contains lubricant sealed into its rollers. These chains last longer than conventional types.

Large rear sprocket

Small front sprocket

Chains and Gearing

To change the gearing of a chain drive machine, the size of the sprockets is altered. A larger rear and smaller front sprocket lower the gearing, giving a lower top speed. A smaller rear and larger front sprocket have the opposite effect.

1904 Quadrant

This early, bicycle-based machine uses chain drive from the engine to the back wheel, and shaft drive from the pedals.

Alternative final-drive cog

Bicycle frame with clipped-on motor parts

Shaft drive from pedals

Shaft Drive

Shaft drive is clean, quiet, and needs no maintenance. There are however, a few drawbacks. The effect of the pinion gear constantly trying to climb up the crown wheel can affect the handling. A machine with its engine mounted across the frame, requires two power-sapping 90° bends in the drive train. Finally, shaft drive is more expensive.

Plunger rear suspension

Universal joints in the shaft allow for suspension movement

Chassis

MOTORCYCLE-CHASSIS DESIGN grew out of pedal bicycle technology. Even after 100 years of development, motorcycle design is still tied to the principles of its predecessor. Today's high-output engines expose the limitations of bicycle-inspired frames, forcing designers to explore new concepts and materials. All areas of the chassis affect the "handling" of a motorbike: an unquantifiable area that concerns the subjective "feel" of a bike that is being ridden. The chassis maintains the distance between the wheels; to maintain optimum handling this must be as constant as possible. Also, chassis flexing must be kept to a minimum, the centre of gravity low, and weight minimized.

The Basic Formula
Although a number of details of design and materials may vary, the basic structure of most motorcycles remains the same. Fashion also plays a part in design decisions: the 1985 Honda VF750, below, uses square-section steel tubing, which has no great engineering merit, and has since fallen from favour. Areas of particular stress on a motorcycle frame are the steering head and the rear swing-arm.

Rear sub-frame supports seat and shock-absorber mounting

Single suspension unit

Braced headstock

Front fork yokes with minimal offset

Swingarm pivot

Box-section tubing

Box-section swingarm

Rear brake torque arm

Rubber-mounted fuel tank

Frame-mounted fairing

Twin front discs

The Honda below is the same model as the one above, but with the bodywork fitted.

Honda VF750

As well as maintaining the distance between the wheels, the frame serves as a structure to hang various components from. Fairings, mudguards, fuel tank, and the seat, are all easily removable to allow access to essential parts such as the engine and gearbox unit. This is bolted firmly in place, providing the chassis with additional rigidity.

Single rear disc brake

Bike Geometry

The dimensions and geometry of a bike have a pronounced effect on its handling. Different combinations of wheelbase, steering-head angle, and trail affect the stability and cornering of the machine. Less trail, caused by narrowing the steering head angle, or by increasing the offset of the forks, gives the bike less straight-line stability but more responsive steering. Shortening the wheelbase has a similar effect.

Steering angle

Fork offset

Trail

HEYSERCYCLE

The aerodynamics of most motorcycles are very poor. The machine below was constructed in 1983, in what became a successful attempt to set a fuel-economy record in America. The all-enveloping aerodynamic bodywork helped the Heysercycle travel the United States coast-to-coast, on less than 15 gallons (68 litres) of fuel, achieving an incredible average of 210 mpg (74.3 km/l).

Indicators are faired in

Aerodynamic canopy

Exhaust

Drag is minimized by covering all protrusions

The Heysercycle was based on a Yamaha four-stroke single. It achieved the record using a sealed fuel tank.

The two chassis tubes start at the headstock, wrap around beneath the engine and return

Norton Road Holder telescopic forks

Twin suspension units

The Norton Featherbed Frame

Introduced in 1950, this frame was many years ahead of its time. The design set new standards in motorcycle handling and improved rider comfort. Even the tubular frames of the 1990s originate from this design. It was given its nickname because of the improvement in the ride quality that it gave.

Tubular swingarm

Chassis spars wrap around the engine

Robust headstock location

Rising-rate linkage

'Upside down' forks

Yamaha FZR1000

Typical of many modern designs, this Yamaha FZR utilizes a twin-spar layout wrapped around the engine. This structure provides maximum rigidity, low centre-of-gravity, and easy access to the engine for maintenance. The spars of this type of frame are made of separate pressed-steel, or lightweight alloy, sections welded together.

Suspension

THE SUSPENSION SERVES two functions. It isolates the main structure of the bike from road surface irregularities, this makes the rider more comfortable and helps prevent the bike shaking to pieces. It also keeps the wheels in contact with the road; an airborne wheel is unable to transmit any braking, steering, or power. Springs separate the main mass of the bike, called the sprung mass, from the wheels and auxiliaries, called the unsprung mass. However, if the bike just sat on springs, it would bounce up and down uncontrollably, so the movement is controlled by a damper that absorbs some of the springs' energy, and also prevents it extending beyond its static position. Damping works on both the compression and the rebound stroke of the spring.

The Spring/Damper Unit

Most bike suspension systems use a coil spring and a hydraulic oil damper (below and left). At the front, the spring and damper are incorporated in a telescopic fork, while the rear uses one or two self-contained units. The operating principle is the same for both. As the spring is compressed, its speed is controlled by the rate at which the oil can pass through holes inside the damper. The speed can be varied by changing the thickness of the oil or the size of the holes.

Suspension units change kinetic energy into heat energy; hard use can result in the oil over-heating and damping loss.

Flexible rubber mounting bush

Twin-rate springs have tightly-wound coils that compress more easily than the wider spaced coils

Damper

The volume or type of gas, effects the springs' compression rate

Pre-load adjuster varies ride-height according to load

Hydraulic-fluid chamber

Flexible rubber mounting bush

Suspension should compress easily at first, to absorb small bumps, then progressively harden to prevent "bottoming out"

A small amount of compressible gas in the chamber allows for the displacement of the incoming rod

Non-return valves allow varying speeds of compression and rebound damping

REAR VARIATIONS

The rear suspension is almost always by swinging arm (actually a swinging fork), that pivots from the rear of the frame, behind the gearbox. Locations and geometric configurations of the shock absorber mounting vary in order to achieve more effective suspension.

Frame

Suspension unit

Rear swingarm

1. CONVENTIONAL LAYOUT
With twin suspension units, one either side of the wheel, this simple, reliable, and cheap layout, offers acceptable performance for road bikes under normal conditions.

Frame

Suspension unit

Rear swingarm

2. CANTILEVER LAYOUT
This moves the shock absorber towards the centre of the machine, offering the potential of increased suspension travel, so is often used on trials bikes. It also means the rear subframe of the bike can be less substantial.

Frame

Rear swingarm

Suspension unit

3. RISING RATE LINKAGE
Used on most competition machines, this arrangement offers the best performance potential. Linkage layout varies, but basically a changing leverage ratio at the suspension unit makes it progressively firmer when compressed.

The Telescopic Fork

Front suspension has a difficult task. With a conventional chassis the braking force is transmitted through the forks; when the brakes are applied, the forks compress. This takes up available suspension travel, and also upsets the chassis geometry. With a conventional chassis the forces generated by braking are very severe, leading to problems with stability and steering when applied. The telescopic fork is almost universally used on modern machines; this was not always the case, and it probably will not last, given the design's severe limitations. (See *Bimota Hub-centre Steering* below.)

Suzuki RGV Grand Prix (below)

A recent development to increase the strength of the fork, is to reverse the relationship of the internal/external components. On a set of "upside down" telescopic forks, the larger tubes are attached to the fork yokes, and the smaller diameter tubes are attached to the wheel. This gives greater fork-strength and more predictable handling when braking.

Large fork tube

Disc-brake and mudguard mounting assembly

Internal slider

Yamaha YZ250 Motocross (below)

Telescopic forks have not changed in principal since they were first used on motorcycles. The legs are comprised of a slider and a tube, within which are the spring, damper rod, oil, and air. As the slider moves up, the spring is compressed, and the oil displaced. The Yamaha, below (also see pages 128-9), has a typical set-up, but with extended forks for motocross use. The YZ250 was the first Japanese production model to use a cantilever rear-suspension system, mounting the long rear suspension unit beneath the fuel tank. This set-up gives the extra suspension travel and ride-height necessary for off-road competition.

De Carbon rear suspension unit

Lightweight rear subframe

Top yoke

Braced headstock

Bottom yoke

Small-diameter fork tube

Dust caps

Large-diameter slider

Triangulated swingarm

Bimota Hub-centre Steering (below)

A more radical approach to front-suspension design, is to separate the processes of braking and steering. With hub-centre steering, the forces generated by the application of the brakes are directed backwards to the frame, rather than upwards, so the suspension is not compressed. As the front springs do not have to resist braking loads, they can be softer and hence more effective in dealing with road bumps. The hub-centre steering concept is not new, but specialist manufacturer Bimota was the first to build a production machine – Yamaha have since followed their lead.

Lightweight aluminium frame plate

Handlebars control the steering by linkage

Braking-torque arm transfers braking loads to the frame

Alloy swingarm

Suspension unit is compressed by swingarm linkage

181

Wheels, Brakes & Tyres

THE MOTORCYCLE AND THE ROAD meet at the tyre; sophisticated braking systems and high power outputs are worthless if the tyre will not grip the road properly. The back tyre of a 500cc Grand Prix bike must deliver 170-brake horsepower through a contact patch the size of a human hand. Such bikes also need effective braking. Developments in engine technology have, of necessity, been mirrored by advances in brake systems. Many new tyre and brake designs originate from successful race bike innovations, having a knock-on effect on production bikes.

Wayne Gardner (above), using special wet-weather race tyres at the British Grand Prix.

A dummy rim-brake of the type fitted to some early machines, this one is from a BSA Model E. This was one of a number of bizarre, and generally ineffective, braking systems that were used on early motorcycles.

The standard front brake assembly used on the early Triumph Trident is a twin leading-shoe drum brake. Drum brakes had been used for fifty years before disc brakes began to take over.

A typical front disc-brake system. The assembly below is from a racing Kawasaki ZX750. Two discs per wheel with twin-piston callipers is now quite common on large, fast machines such as this one.

Cantilever fork

Dummy rim

Twin leading-shoe drum

Chromed-steel rim

Three-spoke alloy wheels

Flexible brake-fluid hose

Calliper unit

Discs are slotted for cooling

Tubeless radial: tyre for a sports bike rear wheel.

Tubeless sports: radial for a front wheel.

Dual purpose rear: road and trail tyre.

Trials tyre: knobbly tread, run at very low pressures.

Drum brakes

Until the 1970s, drum brakes were the norm. This simple and effective design basically consists of two semi-circular brake shoes, that rub against a circular drum in the centre of the wheel. The operating arm, actuated by the brake cable, turns a cam, which forces the two shoes outward against the drum. The shoes are lined with high-friction material that wears away with use. The torque arm prevents the whole mechanism turning when used.

Torque arm

Air-cooling scoop

Operating arm

Speedometer drive cavity

Brake shoe

Brake shoe return spring

High-friction material

Operating cam

Disc brakes

First used on a production motorbike in 1968 by Honda, on their CB 750 (pp. 114-115). The standard hydraulic disc brake operates by two pads, seated in a calliper unit, gripping a disc. The disc is attached to the wheel, and runs between the pads, these are forced together in a pincer movement by the hydraulic-fluid-operated pistons. It has the advantages over a drum brake of being consistently effective (not fading at speed), and needing less frequent, and simpler, maintenance.

The operating parts of a disc-brake system are shown right. Brake fluid cannot be compressed; this gives a smooth and effective braking action.

Brake-fluid reservoir

Piston

Master cylinder

Operating push-rod controlled by the brake-lever

Hydraulic brake fluid

Disc-brake pads are steel blocks lined with high-friction material, which often contains asbestos. They are operated by pressure from fluid-driven pistons (see diagram right).

Holes for locking pins

High-friction material

Tabs help to keep the pads in position

Wheel disc-attached at the hub

Calliper unit

Piston

Brake pad

Standard: general-use tyre for lightweight machines.

Racing intermediate: soft compound with tread for use in variable conditions.

Racing wet: block pattern has channels that force water outwards.

Racing slick: no tread pattern, maximum contact in dry conditions.

Electrics & Instruments

ELECTRICITY IN THE IGNITION SYSTEM has always played a crucial role in the function of the internal combustion engine, and today is additionally used to power an increasing array of components and accessories – once deemed superfluous, but now seen as essential. Power for the ignition system fitted to early engines, was provided by crude batteries. Acetylene was used for lighting, gradually being superseded by electric lighting from 1905 onwards. Since then, electrical systems have been getting increasingly reliable, though more complex. The development of the microchip has heralded a new age of technological sophistication effecting every machine, and the motorbike is no exception.

Sidelight

Horn unit

Twin-head light unit

Lighting
In most countries legislation demands that motorcycles are equipped with indicators. Before the appearance of Japanese machines in the 1960s, these were very unusual. This bike is fitted with twin headlights mounted behind a single lens. Some modern touring machines run electrical accessories as diverse as radio/cassette players, air compressors, and heated handlebar grips.

The Wiring Loom
A motorbike has to cram many components into a very small space. The wiring loom contains hundreds of feet of colour-coded wire, sheathed in plastic insulation for safety, weatherproofing, and to save space. Snap-together joints ensure an electrically safe and weatherproof connection; where necessary they are also rubber-shrouded. An electrical fire, caused by a short-circuit or faulty wiring can destroy a loom in seconds.

Indicator units have flexible mountings, to prevent their breakage in the event of a minor collision

Multi-point connector

Snap connector

Battery

Tail light unit

Transistorized ignition control box

Sealed-for-life
Many electrical components fitted to the modern motorcycle are of a "sealed-for-life" design. This means that the unit has been designed to be maintenance-free during its working life. Some of these components may well last as long as the machine itself; however, parts such as flasher units, electronic ignition units, and sealed-beam headlamps, may need replacing over the years. The disposable nature of these items is berated by some, but being sealed and tamper-proof can result in greater long-term reliability.

Voltage regulator

Fuses

Flasher unit

Brake-light switch

Rear indicator unit

GENERATORS
When the engine is running, power is supplied to the battery by a generator – usually mounted on the end of the crankshaft – and from there to the electrical components. There are two types of generators: the alternator and the dynamo. The alternator generates alternating current (a.c.); the dynamo, fitted to older bikes, produces direct current (d.c.). The alternator's output is converted to d.c., so it can feed the battery, by a rectifier. Both require a regulator to control the current produced, as demand dictates.

Dial shows miles- and kilometres-per-hour

Cable-driven worm gear

The needle rises or falls according to how much current passes through the engine sensor

Odometer

Tripmeter

A compact and delicate mechanism drives this multi-purpose unit

Gauges and Warning Lights

Accurate instrumentation keeps the rider informed of speed, mileage, engine revs, and water temperature. By knowing the engine's running temperature and speed, overheating can be averted. This may prevent a costly and dangerous engine seizure. Warning lights also alert the rider of oil-pressure loss and generator failure.

Inside the speedometer

The speedometer, tripmeter, and odometer, are combined in one cable-driven, mechanical unit.

Electric temperature gauges fitted to water-cooled engines, have a thermo-electric sensor in the cooling system. This allows current to flow from the gauge, according to the water's temperature.

Rev counters used to be mechanical but now operate by using the interrupted electrical signal on the low-tension side of the coil (see p.175). This is converted into a readable magnetic signal.

Headlight dip switch

Indicator switch

Horn switch

Left-hand multi-switch unit

Coil

Ignition switch and lock

Main section of wiring loom

Branch section of wiring loom

Flexibly mounted front indicator unit

Headlamp unit containing two lights

Coil

High-tension lead to spark plug

Right-hand multi-switch unit

Starter switch

Headlight-and sidelight-on switch

Engine-kill switch

Headlamp bulb

The Rider's Clothing

MOTORCYCLISTS NEED TO PROTECT themselves particularly well against the weather. At first, riders used a bizarre assortment of clothing originally intended for cycling and horse riding. Special clothing was not needed; early machines were not much faster than horses, and they usually broke down in the rain. As bikes improved so did riding gear. Modern crash helmets must withstand impacts at high speeds; eyes must be protected with a visor or goggles; sturdy, calf-length boots are worn (different types of riding, such as motocross and racing, require different boots). Gloves must keep the hands warm without impairing their ability to operate controls.

The American racer
Dave Aldana caused controversy by wearing these spectacular skeleton leathers in the early seventies. He had another set that were a copy of Superman's outfit.

The collar must be well designed to keep the rider warm and dry

Reinforced Synthetic Jacket
Traditional waterproof clothing offered minimal protection in the event of an accident. Modern suits may incorporate body-armour in critical locations, like the elbows and shoulders. This suit is made of Gore-tex, a man-made fabric that allows moisture from inside to escape while keeping the rain out.

Glass lens goggles do not scratch and are laminated for safety

Elbow pads are made of a dense foam material. They are inserted into pockets in the elbow

Wide flaps cover the zips to protect against wind and water

Winter gloves need to be very thermally efficient. Thin metal foil is used to keep the heat in without making the glove excessively bulky

An open-face crash helmet with detachable peak

Knee-pads are incorporated into the trousers

Many riders still prefer "open-face" or "jet" helmets despite the fact that they offer no protection for the face in the event of an accident. However, they do have the advantage of being cooler in hot conditions. Eye protection is provided by goggles, a visor, or glasses.

General purpose motorcycle boots need to be strong and comfortable, with protection for the shins as well as the ankles and toes. Racers use less durable lightweight boots for extra sensitivity to the controls.

Early attempts at head protection.

Before the development of glass-fibre and plastic, helmets were made from canvas, cork, and leather. They afforded no protection to the side of the head.

Enduring leather
For protection, leather remains the best material. This is supplemented by hard foam padding on the shoulders, elbows, back, and knees.

Touring riders favour the versatile two-piece leather suit over the one-piece racing leather. The jacket and trousers can be joined with a zip

Studded palm gloves slide in contact with the road, rather than shredding

Some areas are elasticated, giving flexibility to allow for movement of the knees, elbows, and back

— RACING PROTECTION —

Carl Fogarty (left) demonstrates the technique for grinding down knee sliders on the TT course. When he has destroyed them, they are removed and replaced.

Modern road racers slide their knees along the ground when cornering; sliders were developed in response to this technique. "Knee-down" provides racers with more information about their speed and lean angle. It can also help them to save a slide.

The hard nylon sliders are ground away by contact with the track

A black leather jacket was part of the uniform of the Rockers, a youth movement of the 1950s. This factor and the use of leathers in films that featured stars like Marlon Brando and James Dean, helped to give the impression that leather jackets were worn by the glamorous and/or dangerous.

Full-face Crash Helmets
These helmets have a shell made from plastic or glass-fibre, with an energy-absorbing liner. After an accident, a helmet must be replaced as the liner will have been compressed, destroying its protective qualities.

Replaceable anti-scratch visor

The leather biker's jacket, once a symbol of rebellion, is now universally worn, often by non-motorcyclists. Bikers adopted leather because it is windproof, durable, protects the rider in the event of a fall, and moulds itself into the wearer's shape. It is still widely used by motorcyclists because of its protective qualities.

Glossary

Words in italic within an entry have their own entry in the glossary.

AMA American Motorcyclists' Association.

ATMOSPHERIC INLET VALVE Inlet valve which is opened by the vacuum in the cylinder created by the falling piston. Commonly used on early machines.

BELLMOUTH Air intake trumpet attached to the carburettor.

BHP Brake Horse Power, a measurement of the engine's maximum power output.

BORE Measurement of the width of a cylinder, usually expressed in millimetres.

CAM Rotating eccentric used to control valve or *ignition timing*, also used to operate drum-brakes.

CARBURETTOR Instrument for mixing fuel and air into a combustible vapour.

CHAIR A sidecar. A motorcycle fitted with a sidecar can also be known as an *outfit* or *combination*.

CLINCHER RIMS Type of rim used with some early inflatable tyres.

CLIP-ONS Sports or racing handlebars that are clamped low onto the fork legs.

CONTACT BREAKER Switch in the low tension ignition circuit, controlling timing of the spark in the high tension circuit.

CRADLE Motorcycle frame which places the engine between two frame tubes. See also *open cradle* and *stressed member*.

CRANKSHAFT The critical part of the engine which changes the linear movement of the piston into rotational movement.

CONSTANT LOSS The system of lubrication or ignition in which there is no circuit for the oil or electricity to return to the oil tank or the battery.

DOHC Double overhead camshafts.

DISTRIBUTOR Ignition system device on some multi-cylinder engines that sends the high-tension spark to the correct cylinder.

EARLES FORKS *Leading-link* forks designed by Ernie Earles, at one time favoured by BMW. Also called long *leading-link* forks.

FAIRING An front enclosure to improve the bike's aerodynamics or the rider's comfort.

FIM Federation International Motorcyclists – the governing body of international motor-cycle sport.

FLAT/HORIZONTALLY OPPOSED ENGINE Engine layout in which the cylinders are placed at 180° to one another.

FLOAT BOWL The *carburettor* fuel reservoir into which the flow of fuel is controlled by a valve operated by a float.

GIRDER FORKS A common form of front suspension on early machines. The front wheel is held in a set of forks which are attached to the steering head by parallel links.

IGNITION TIMING Refers to the position of the piston or *crankshaft* when the spark occurs, relative to *TDC*. Usually expressed in degrees.

INLET MANIFOLD Tube connecting the *carburettor* to the inlet port.

IOE Inlet over exhaust. Valve layout in which the inlet valve is placed directly above the (side) exhaust valve. Common on early engines, a development of atmospheric valve engines.

LEADING-LINK Front suspension system in which short links pivot at the bottom of a solid fork. The axle mounts on the front of the link, movement of which is controlled by a spring.

LEADING SHOE The first of the two shoes to encounter the rotating drum when braking.

MAG ALLOY Lightweight magnesium alloy.

MEGAPHONE A tapered performance exhaust.

OHC Overhead camshaft.

OHV Overhead valve. The valves are placed above the combustion chamber and opened by *pushrods* from a low camshaft.

OPEN CRADLE A frame which has no lower frame tubes: the engine is bolted into place becoming part of the frame as a *stressed member* (the frame is incomplete without the engine).

PLUNGER Rear suspension system where the axle is mounted between two vertical springs.

PORT Passage or opening leading to the interior of the cylinder.

PORT TIMING The moment when the ports are masked or unmasked in a two-stroke engine.

PRESSED STEEL Sheet steel pressed into rigid shapes that are welded together to make frames.

PRE-UNIT Engine and gearbox constructed in separate units, common on older machines.

PRIMARY DRIVE The unit which transfers power from the engine to the clutch/gearbox.

PRIVATEERS Racers without factory support.

PUSHRODS Rods that transmit the lift of the camshaft lobes to the tappets in *OHV* engines.

REAR SETS Racing footrests, placed further toward the rear of the bike than usual, to allow the rider to adopt a prone position.

SENDER Component that conveys information about the engine to a gauge or warning light.

SIDE VALVE Positioning of the valves beside the cylinder.

SNAIL CAM CHAIN ADJUSTERS Helical shaped *cams* mounted on the axle to allow accurate chain adjustment.

SOHC Single overhead camshaft

SPINE (frame) A frame whose main structure connects the steering head and swingarm pivot, with the engine suspended beneath it.

STRESSED MEMBER Component (usually the engine) that forms part of the whole structure (usually the frame).

STROKE Measurement of the piston's travel, usually expressed in millimetres.

SUPERCHARGER Device for compressing the engine's incoming charge.

TT Tourist Trophy races at the Isle of Man.

TDC Top Dead Centre (or 0°) – the point when the *crankshaft* and piston are at the uppermost in their travel.

TIMING Measurement of the position of the valves, piston or *crankshaft* relative to the *stroke* of the piston or revolution of the crankshaft. See also *port* and *ignition timing*.

TOMMY BAR A short tool used for levering.

TRAILING-LINK Similar to *leading link* forks, except the link pivots at the front with the axle mounted at the rear.

TWINPORT A cylinder head design that has two ports branching away from a single valve.

UNIT CONSTRUCTION Construction of the engine and gearbox within the same casings.

UNSPRUNG WEIGHT The weight of parts of the machine that are not sprung. i.e. wheels, tyres, brakes, fork sliders, front mudguard etc.

V-TWIN Engine layout in which the cylinders are placed in a "V" formation.

WORKS RACERS Factory racing machines.

ZENER DIODE A type of voltage regulator.

Index

Motorcycles are listed chronologically under the names of their manufacturers.

Acknowledgments

The Author's acknowledgments
This book would not have been possible without the help of many people. First and foremost, thanks go to the motorcycle museums – the Motorcycle Heritage Museum of Westerville, Ohio, the National Motorcycle Museum of Birmingham, the National Motor Museum of Beaulieu, Hants, the Sammy Miller Museum of New Milton, Hants, and the Deutsches Zweirad-Museum NSU-Museum of Neckarsulm in Germany, and the many individual enthusiasts who have maintained, restored and preserved the motorcycles pictured here. Many went to considerable trouble to enable us to photograph their machines. My gratitude goes to:

Mike Arden, Howard Atkin, George Beale, Leon Blackman, Jim Carlton, Chequered Flag Motocross, Ken Chieffo, Chris Childs, Dr William Cleveland, Peter Collins, John Comerford, Frank Degenero, Al & Pat Doerman, Billy Doyle, Duckhams Oils, Al Fair, Simon Fenning, Surrey Harley-Davidson, Robert Fergus, Galleria Bimota, Tim Geddes, Richard Gerholt, Perry Gotschal, Wilf Green Motorcycles, Russ Harris, Honda of America Marysville Ohio, Honda UK, Dennis Howard, Husky Sport UK, Dave Jones, Peter Jones, Doug Kane, John Lawes, Mike Leach, Don Leason, Kit Lewis, Callaghan at Lewis Leathers London, Bruce Lindsay, Valentine Lindsay, Lucky Strike/Suzuki, Jim McCabe, Cyril Malem, Marlboro Team Roberts, Mark Medarski, Michelin Tyres, Mitsui Yamaha, Pat Morris, Motor Cycle City, Jeff Murphy, Ronald & Lorraine Myers, Mike Olney, Dr John Patt, Tony Penachio, Bruce Penhall, Paul Pierce, Hayden Racknall, Larry Reece, Roger Reiman, Renham Motorcycles, Ed Schmidt, Francis Sheehan, Phil Somerfield, Marion Sosnowski, Frank Stevens, John Surtees, James Sutter, Dennis Trollope, Merrill Vanderslice, Les Williams, Richard Winger, Mort Wood, Charles Wright, John Wynne, Ed Youngblood.

Further thanks for tracking down elusive machines and their owners go to the Vintage Motorcycle Club, The Moto Guzzi Club, the Vintage Japanese Motorcycle Club, the Italian Motorcycle Owners Club, Steve at Motodd, Benji Straw at Weevee, Stuart Lanning of Scootering magazine.

Many people provided information and advice, especially notable contributions were made by Mark Graham, Marcus Allard, Peter Watson, Shed, Phil Heath, Chris Dabbs, Terry Snelling, Adam Duckworth, John Watson-Miller, Prosper Keating, and David Lancaster. Very special thanks go to Jim Rogers of the American Motorcycle Heritage Foundation for his unstinting enthusiasm, encouragement, and co-operation. Also to Steve Jones and Francis for saying the right thing at the right time.

I would also like to thank the following people at Dorling Kindersley for their part in the production of this book. Tracy Hambleton-Miles for patience and persistence in appropriate quantities; Jane Mason and Lol Henderson for their editorial input; Simon Hinchliffe for being solid; Tina Vaughan for being a perfectionist (but I still don't like that Harley); and Sean Moore for overseeing the project. Also Dave King and Jonathan Buckley for taking fine photographs and being excellent company.

This book is dedicated to Lucas and Esther.

Dorling Kindersley would like to thank the following:
Katie John and Stephanie Jackson for editirial assistance; Peter Miles and Tim Streater for additional research; Hugh Ackermann and W.R. Richards of the National Motorcycle Museum, Birmingham; Paul Board and Annice Collett of the National Motor Museum Reference Library, Beaulieu; Eric Brockway; Brian Woolley at EMAP, Peterborough; Phil Heath of the Vintage Motor Cycle Club, Seaham, Co. Durham; Rob Munro-Hall and Kate Anderson at Motor Cycle News, Kettering; Martin Jones, Secretary of the Triumph Owners Club; Sammy Miller; Friedhelm Raatz of the Deutsches Zweirad-Museum NSU-Museum Neckarsulm, Germany; Jim Rogers of the Motorcycle Heritage Museum, Westerville, Ohio; and Jan Smit for technical information; Edward Bunting for translation and research; Simon Murrell and Paula Burgess for additional design assistance; Nicolas Hall and Simon Hinchliffe for artworks; Jane Mason and Jonathan Buckley for modelling; Julia Ruxton for picture research, and Pat Coward for the index.

PICTURE CREDITS
t=top b=bottom c=centre l=left r=right u=under
The American Motorcyclist Magazine, Westerville, Ohio: Endpaper; 22tl; 22tr; 22bl; 23tr; 23cl; 28tl; 28tr; 28c; 30tl; 34tr; 37bc; 50tl; 98tl; 130tl; 131tr; 139cr; 145tl; 148tl; 157cl; 162tl; 163tr.
Deutsches Zweirad-Museum NSU-Museum, Neckarsulm: 59tl.
EMAP Archives, Peterborough: 8br; 38tr; 44tr; 44bl; 45tc; 48tl; 49tl; 52tr; 58tr; 65ucl; 65cr; 66tr; 69tl; 70tl; 73tl; 78cr; 80cr; 81cr; 83tl; 92tr; 97c; 102cr; 102b; 112cr; 140bl; 147tr; 153tc; 159cr: /Martyn Barnwell: 36c.
Mary Evans Picture Library, London: 50tr; 68tl.
Patrick Gosling, London: 145tr; 145cr; 149cr.
Harley-Davidson, Inc., Milwaukee: 18tr; 20cr; 24tl.
Michel Hilderal: 136bl; 136bc.
Honda (UK), London: 112tl.
Hulton Deutsch: 12tr; 29c; 29br; 36cl; 51bc; 64tl.
Kobal Collection, London: 75br.
Stephen Lovell-Davis: 151tc.
Lucky Strike/Suzuki, Edenbridge: 146tr.
Michel Lepage: 137tl; 137tr.
Magnum Photos/Chris Steele-Perkins: 99c.
Metalurgia Casal, Portugal: 141cr; 141br.
Don Morley: 118tl; 134bl; 147cr; 150tr; 153cr; 155br; 158tr; 159tl; 159tc; 163tc; 163cr; 163br; 164tl; 165cl; 187tc.
Moto Guzzi, GBM S.p.A., Mandello del Lario, Italy: 100tl.
Motor Cycle News, Kettering: 61bl; 76tl; 90tr; 94tl; 106tl; 115c; 119bc; 119br; 121tr; 123tl; 140cr; 141c; 144tr; 151cr; 154tr; 155tc; 156tl; 156cl; 157tl; 157c; 157cr; 160tr; 166tr; 166cr; 167tr; 167cr; 182tr; 186tr.
National Motor Museum, Beaulieu: 8bl; 10tc; 10tr; 11tl; 11tcr; 11tr; 13 bl; 51c; 76cr; 79tr; 87tl; 124tr; 136tl; 138bl; 147tc; 152tr; 153tl; 153tr; 164cr.
Popperfoto: 187cr.
Rescue Photography: 78cl.
Science Museum Photo Library, London: 8tr; 9tr.
SP Tyres UK Ltd: 11tc.
Sporting Pictures UK: 159tr; 161tl; 161cl.
John Surtees, Edenbridge: 104tr.
Oli Tennent, London: 149tr.
Triumph Motorcycles, Hinckley: 76br.
R. & M. Walker, Cambridge: 90tl; 91tl; 97bc; 97br.
World's Motorcycle News Agency: 137c; 140cl.